OPEN
RETURN

May I never boast of anything except
the cross of our Lord Jesus Christ,
by which the world has been
crucified to me, and I to the world

(Galatians 6.14)

OPEN RETURN

Renewing your faith through
the Gospel story

Roy Williamson

An Draw
beloved friend
and colleague

Roy

TRIANGLE

First published in Great Britain in 2000 by
Triangle
Society for Promoting Christian Knowledge
Holy Trinity Church
Marylebone Road
London NW1 4DU

Unless otherwise stated Bible references are from
The New Revised Standard Version of the Bible © 1989.

British Library Cataloguing-in-Publication Data

A catalogue record for this book is available from
the British Library

ISBN 0–281–05292–1

Typeset by Pioneer Associates, Perthshire
Printed in Great Britain by
Omnia Books Ltd, Bishopbriggs, Glasgow

Contents

To my grandchildren
Michael, Robert, Danny,
Emily, Rachel, Edward and Henry
who keep me sane, warm my heart
and make me laugh.

I am grateful to my editor Alison Barr
for her wise advice and to Matty McQuillan
and Jonathan Williamson for reading the text
and offering suggestions for improvement.
All biblical quotations are taken from the
New Revised Standard Version.

Introduction

The shape and purpose of this little book have been determined by an ancient monument on the River Shannon in mid-Ireland. The Cross of Clonmacnoise, also known as the Cross of the Scriptures, has stood for over ten centuries during which it has fulfilled a dual purpose. It was a landmark and witness to the Christian faith and it served as a teaching aid to the faithful. Carved into its stone are illustrations of Bible stories which, in past centuries, priests used as visual aids to teach the faith to local people. Its presence is a continuing reminder of the story of faith.

When a friend offered me the gift of a new pectoral cross to mark the beginning of my episcopal ministry in the Diocese of Southwark I asked that it should be modelled on the Cross of the Scriptures and that the stories carved upon it would be those that had particular significance in my own journey of faith.

Again and again I have returned to those stories. On occasions, when under particular pressure and without others realizing I was doing it, I allowed my fingers to trace the story engraved upon the cross and focused my mind on its truth for today. It not only brought me personal strength and encouragement it also reminded me of those foundation truths of the gospel that must be proclaimed afresh in each generation.

Open Return

I have thought frequently of those wayside pilgrims who, centuries ago, were taught the rudiments of the faith for the first time as they stood gazing at the Cross of Clonmacnoise. Many of them, I am sure, would return again and again to renew that faith and draw strength from the story of faith inscribed upon that cross.

It is that thought of returning to the cross as pilgrims that has inspired this book and provided the specific purpose for writing it. An embarrassing moment on a Midland Mainline train served as the catalyst.

'Sir, I'm sorry to tell you, but you're on the wrong train. Your ticket, a supersaver, is not valid on this train. If you wish to continue the journey you must pay an extra charge.' I had bought an off-peak ticket earlier in the day but, foolishly and mistakenly, I was returning on a peak-time train, eager to get home after a day of boring committees. The ticket collector was gracious and understanding. I was embarrassed and apologetic – and have never made the same mistake again. It is now like music to my ears when, having enquired about the validity of the ticket I have just purchased, the railway official assures me, 'It's an open return, sir, you can return at any time, on any train, on any day.'

My purpose in writing this book is to provide an 'open return', a simple, unsophisticated aid for people to renew their acquaintance with the Jesus story and how they may relate to it today.

Like many others, I am conscious of times in life, even retirement life, when I need to stop, stand still and take stock of who I am, what I'm doing and where I'm going – and why! Times when I feel the need to return to base, as it were, to regroup, to remind myself of how it all began and to renew my commitment to the God who is Father, Son and Holy Spirit.

I don't want to study a lengthy theological treatise. I have neither the time nor the inclination to go on a training course or attend a retreat. I don't want to be preached at or counselled. I just want to reflect quietly, at my own pace and in my own time, on the Scriptures and on some foundation truths of the Jesus story. I don't want to be pressurized, I just want to relax and take it a day at a time. I want an 'open return' so that I can, as it were, take up the 'old old story' at a point which may be appropriate for the time of year or which may speak to my present needs and circumstances.

It is not a lackadaisical approach to the faith; on the contrary, it is an attempt to get to grips with some of the fundamentals of the faith in an accessible manner. I know of house groups where such an approach would be helpful. I'm aware of families, who have allowed the spiritual dimension of life to fade from their home, for whom such an approach would provide a new start. There are busy executives who, far from despising such an unsophisticated approach, would welcome it and find time to pause and reflect as opportunity arose in the midst of competing claims on their daily life. Those who were beginning to 'dip their toes' in the waters of faith could find in this approach an informative and unthreatening introduction. Its division into appropriate sections makes it possible for an 'open return' to be made as need and opportunity arise.

The birth, baptism, life, passion, death, resurrection and ascension of Jesus, together with the coming of the Holy Spirit, are the stories engraved on my Cross of the Scriptures. They have historical roots in the past. They bring us face to face with what God the Father intended and made present in history through his Son. With the help of God's faithful and creative Spirit those same stories can touch our lives with relevance and renewing power today.

We possess an 'open return' to the story of God, a God who is ready to welcome us as we are, at any time, on any day, in any place. It is my hope that this little book will serve that end.

I

Joy to the world

Joy to the world, the Lord has come!
let earth receive her King;
let every heart prepare Him room
and heaven and nature sing!

(ANGLICAN HYMN BOOK)

A child on the doorstep

> And she gave birth to her firstborn son
> and wrapped him in bands of cloth, and
> laid him in a manger because there was
> no place for them in the inn.
>
> (LUKE 2.7)

Those who have been fortunate enough to be present at a quality performance of Oscar Wilde's play *The Importance of Being Earnest* will recall that unforgettable exclamation from the lips of Lady Bracknell – 'A handbag!' Spoken by a Maggie Smith or a Dame Edith Evans they draw forth both admiration and applause for the wealth of surprise, indignation and dismay they manage to convey in two such simple words. That a son and heir could be deposited in a handbag and placed in the left-luggage department of a railway station was, to Lady Bracknell, truly astounding.

Yet something even more astonishing took place in Bethlehem just over 2000 years ago. The God of creation placed, as it were, a child, his Son, on the doorstep of the world he planned to rescue. A royal birth in a very unroyal setting.

Frankly, if you or I had plans for saving the world we wouldn't, humanly speaking, have started from here. A proper start in life is so important. Begin as you mean to go on; that's the acquired wisdom of the ages. What hope for the world if the saviour you provide lies helpless on a bed of straw? What chance of rescuing creation if you begin by being banished 'round the back' of a wayside inn, excluded and obscure? How would it look on his CV? – 'Entered this life in obscurity, departed this life in shame'?

Clearly it was not the way to win friends or influence

people. But then, as Isaiah reminds us, God does tend to approach things in a unique way.

> For my thoughts are not your thoughts,
> nor are your ways my ways, says the Lord.
> For as the heavens are higher than the earth,
> so are my ways higher than your ways and
> my thoughts than your thoughts.

> (ISAIAH 55.8, 9)

The picture of a child left on the doorstep has been a familiar story in folklore throughout the ages. It is full of pathos and possibility. It tugs at the heart-strings, it evokes sympathy, it provokes enquiry. Who is this child? Where did he come from? What is his destiny? All proper questions but few bothered to ask them on the night Jesus was born – the crowds in Bethelehem were too preoccupied.

History, however, has supplied some of the answers. The babe lying in straw held infinite possibilities for the whole of creation. Here is the dawn of a new day for the world. Here is God taking flesh and entering into the human situation. Here is God's plan for the ultimate healing of creation. Here, in the babe of Bethlehem, lies the hope of all the ends of the earth. Here is God's gift – what matter where he places it as long as it is received with gratitude and gladness?

> Thou didst leave Thy throne
> and Thy kingly crown,
> when Thou camest to earth for me;
> but in Bethlehem's home
> there was found no room
> for Thy holy nativity.
> O come to my heart, Lord Jesus,
> there is room in my heart for Thee.

> (ANGLICAN HYMN BOOK)

Joy to the world

The story of the infant Son of God left on the doorstep of his world has captivated the imagination of millions throughout the ages. The excessive commercialism that often surrounds the Christmas season tends to trivialize the story and dull its beauty. Nevertheless, it continues to inspire love and transform lives for its power is not in its beauty but in its truth. God so loved the world that he gave his only Son.

A passage to read

Luke 2.1–7.

A thought to ponder upon

Mary holds her finger out, and a divine hand closes on it. The maker of the world is born a begging child; he begs for milk, and does not know that it is milk for which he begs. We will not lift our hands to pull the love of God down to us, but he lifts his hands to pull human compassion down upon his cradle. So the weakness of God proves stronger than men, and the folly of God proves wiser than men.

(A. FARRER, *SAID OR SUNG*, 1976)

A prayer to use

Thanks be to you, O God, for your indescribable gift of Jesus.

(2 CORINTHIANS 9.15)

A young woman and God

Then Mary said, 'Here am I, the servant
of the Lord; let it be with me according to
your word.'

(LUKE 1.38)

When God placed a child, his Son, on the doorstep of his
world, it was his way of saying 'Yes' to the whole of his
creation and, in particular, to all humankind. Could he have
paid them a greater compliment than becoming man?

God's great 'Yes' to the world, however, was made possible only because of another 'Yes' that came from the lips
of a young Jewish woman. Through her joyful response to
God's initiative the way was opened for Jesus to be born as
the Saviour of the world.

It all began when the young woman, Mary by name, was
engaged to Joseph. She received a visit from the messenger
of God, Gabriel by name, who assured her of two things;
she was highly favoured and God was with her. That was
all very well but when you're not expecting a personally
delivered message from God, it comes as a bit of a shock.
Mary was more than a touch perplexed, she was fearful.
Visitations from God often included an element of judgement.
Assurance was one thing but reassurance was another and,
in view of the unexpected visitor and the news he brought,
it was the latter she needed most – especially in the light of
what was to come.

'Don't be afraid, Mary', came the reassuring words, followed by what surely must be the most amazing revelation
that any human being has ever heard concerning their
future. Though a virgin, she would conceive, bear a son and
name him Jesus. Hers would be no ordinary conception, it
would come about through the 'overshadowing' of the Holy

Spirit. And Jesus would be no ordinary child, for he would be called the Son of God and reign over a kingdom that would never end. How's that for a surprise announcement?

It wasn't just surprising, of course, it was absolutely shattering. It placed strain on her relationship with Joseph. It opened up the possibility of innuendo and suspicion. And, as later events proved, it introduced her to a responsibility which, whatever its undoubted privilege and joy, would end in a broken heart.

Her response to the messenger of God was awaited. So much depended on it. What if she had said 'No'? Could she have said, 'No'? Mary's answer, when it came, put such speculative and hypothetical questions firmly in their place. 'Here am I, the servant of the Lord; let it be with me according to your word.' In other words, she placed herself entirely at God's disposal. Her answer revealed no reluctant compliance with the will of God, no indication that this amazing gift of God's Spirit was being foisted upon her. On the contrary, the original language suggests an eagerness to receive God's gift and to be a part of God's plan.

Thus Mary became the mother of the Son of God, the immediate source of Jesus' human existence. God chose an insignificant person for dignity and greatness. Israel's hope and Israel's destiny are realized as a new human life begins in the body of a young Jewish woman of no importance. Mary, in her great Song of Praise, Magnificat, described God as one who 'lifted up the lowly'. It was true, wonderfully true, in her experience, and we are to take encouragement and inspiration from it.

We are unlikely to have a spectacular visitation from the Archangel Gabriel but God never ceases to be active in his world and in that particular community to which we belong. As he revealed in his dealings with Mary, he is prepared and eager to offer ordinary, humble people a share in that activity and to use them in fulfilling his purposes for the well-being of his whole creation.

There is a sense in which Mary, thankfully receiving God's great gift, nurtured it in her body and then shared it with the world. It is a pattern to follow. Lives placed at the disposal of God not only receive blessing but in turn give blessing to others.

A passage to read

Luke 1.26–38.

A thought to ponder upon

Holiness consists in doing the will of God with a smile.

(MOTHER TERESA, QUOTED IN WARD AND WILD, 1997)

A prayer to use

Almighty God,
as you looked upon the holiness and humility
of the Blessed Virgin Mary
and chose her to be the mother of your only Son:
give us, like her, an eagerness to place ourselves at
your disposal and to share your gifts of love and
   grace with
others that, together, we may know your joy
   and blessing.

Glory in the fields

Then an angel of the Lord stood before
them and the glory of the Lord shone
around them, and they were terrified

(LUKE 2.9)

Boredom rather than glory may have been uppermost in the
minds of the shepherds that night as they watched over their
sheep outside Bethlehem. Life under the stars in Palestinian
fields can be a rather chilly experience as the blistering heat
of day gives way to bitter cold of night. It is true, as the
Psalmist maintained, that the heavens declare the glory of
God, but there's a limit to the fascination of the stars when
faced with them every night of the year. Besides they were
paid to watch sheep, not stars.

Suddenly, all that changed. Sheep, stars, cold, even the
possibility of marauders attacking their flocks, were all
forgotten in a moment of sheer terror. An angel of the Lord
unexpectedly appeared before them and the glory of the
Lord surrounded them. No wonder they were thunderstruck!
So would I have been, in their position.

They would have known, from stories of their patriarchs,
that the presence of the glory of God was cause neither for
comfort nor complacency. When the Tabernacle, which
stood at the heart of Jewish worship, was enveloped by a
dazzling light, it symbolized the presence of God. The dazzling light was a sign of God's glory. More often than not it
was also an indication that people should keep their distance. But here they were, probably too terrified to move,
with a heavenly visitor in front of them and the dazzling
light of God's glory all round them. It must have been a bit
scary.

Which is why, I am sure, the angel immediately tried to
put them at their ease. Don't be afraid, the news is good.

11

There is joy for you and all the people. The Messiah, the one you have been hoping for and looking for, has arrived. The Saviour of the world has been born this very day and, 'as a sign, you will find him wrapped in bands of cloth and lying in a manger'.

Given the declared Messianic status of the new arrival and his unique role *vis à vis* the world, they could have expected a more impressive sign. Instead, the Saviour, Christ and Lord, is to be found lying in an animal's feeding trough, his arrival as common as any other child born to the poor.

It was the conception of Jesus that was unique. There was nothing unique about either his birth or the fact that he lay in a manger. The shepherds, perhaps, had seen other newly born children lying on a bed of straw. Perhaps this was the true importance of 'the sign'. Luke, when writing his Gospel record, reveals a special concern for the poor and outcasts of society. The child in the animal's feeding trough is the Saviour of the world, and the blessings which he brings, unlike so many other benefits in that day and age, will not be denied to the poor. From the very beginning he is identified with them.

But the night of surprises wasn't over. The sign might have been something of an anti-climax but now they were given the full treatment. The angel was joined by massed choirs from heaven singing the Glory Song:

> Glory to God in the highest heaven,
> and on earth peace among those
> whom he favours.

They couldn't wait to get to Bethlehem to check it all out. No sooner had the angelic choir gone home when they hurried to the stable and found Mary and Joseph watching over the baby in the manger. They told everyone, including Mary and Joseph, what had happened in the fields. People were amazed and the shepherds, with hearts filled with praise to God for all that they had seen and heard, returned to the mundane task of minding their sheep – after all, that was where God had revealed his glory to them.

There is an interesting paradox here. Perhaps it was one of the things Mary pondered in her heart as the shepherds returned. She and Joseph knew nothing about the massed choir of angels and the Glory Song until the shepherds told them. No visitors from heaven for them as they got on with the tasks of childbirth in difficult conditions. But theirs was the baby. And he was 'Emmanuel' – God with us. That was glory indeed.

A passage to read

Luke 2.8–20.

A thought to ponder upon

> Thou who wast rich beyond all splendour,
> All for love's sake becamest poor;
> Thrones for a manger didst surrender,
> Sapphire-paved courts for stable floor.
> Thou who wast rich beyond all splendour,
> All for love's sake becamest poor.

(BP F. HOUGHTON, 1934, ANGLICAN HYMN BOOK)

A prayer to use

> God of surprises,
> keep us faithful but never complacent
>   in the work you have called us to do.
> May we always be open to glimpses of your
>   glory in the world around us.

Guidance in the sky

In the time of King Herod, after Jesus was born in Bethlehem of Judea, wise men from the East came to Jerusalem, asking, 'Where is the child who has been born king of the Jews? For we observed his star at its rising, and have come to pay him homage.'

(MATTHEW 2.1, 2)

God meets people where they are. That was true of the shepherds. The glory of God shone around them as they went about their business of minding sheep. It was also true of the wise men or, Magi, as they are called. They were students of the stars and apparently gained insights into world affairs from their studies. It was in that astrological realm, it seems, that God spoke to them in language they could understand. Whatever that phenomenon was, they discerned that the Jewish expectation of a coming king had been fulfilled. They saw it in the stars, 'We have seen his star at its rising.'

They followed their insights and their instincts and went searching for the new-born king. Quite naturally they assumed that a Jewish king would be born in the capital city, so they came to Jerusalem. There they were told by Herod the King, who hid his own sinister agenda beneath a superficial expression of goodwill, that they would find the child in Bethlehem. So they set out for Bethlehem, guided by the star, 'until it stopped over the place where the child was'.

I don't think that the story requires us to believe that the star travelled at camel speed and at rooftop height all the way from the East to the lodgings of Mary and Joseph. But it seems likely that the special star which they had seen at its rising, and which marked the beginning of their journey, now appeared again to indicate the end of their search and the beginning of a unique experience. They had arrived at their destination and, perhaps, came face to face with their destiny.

To say they were pleased would be a massive under-statement. They were delighted, overwhelmed with joy. Entering the house they saw the child with Mary his mother. They knelt down and, with Eastern custom, touched the ground with their heads as a sign of homage and submission. Then opening their treasure chests, they offered him gifts of gold, frankincense and myrrh. Then they went home, but by a different route in order to avoid Herod.

After such a long journey the record of their encounter with the infant king appears incredibly brief. But, of course, the purpose of Matthew, the writer, is not to go into the minute details of a visit that may have lasted for days. He doesn't even expand on the nature and significance of the gifts. Over the years preachers have been less reticent on this matter and some, with vivid imagination and bold conjecture, have come up with suggestions that leave one breathless! I believe that the costly nature of the gifts indi-cates that the wise men were wealthy people and that they offered their best to this special child.

Matthew seems more concerned, as it were, with the big picture. He wants to draw attention to the significance of this royal child. He is not just the king of the Jews, he is the king of the whole world. The Magi's insights and instincts were absolutely right in following the star and in falling down to worship this infant king.

When God called Abraham centuries before, it was in order to make him the father of a great nation, Israel. Israel, in turn, was meant to be a blessing to the whole world. It didn't quite turn out like that, however, and Israel became more and more exclusive. Nevertheless, it was always God's intention that Israel should be a light to the Gentiles and that they would be attracted to that light. With the birth of Jesus Christ that purpose of God was about to be perfectly fulfilled. That is the primary significance of the coming of the wise men to the infant king at Bethlehem. They symbolize the coming of the Gentiles to the light of Christ. The homage they gave Jesus was a sign that they recognized not only the universality of his kingship but also that God's purposes are to be fulfilled in him. They are responsive to both.

The wise men began a journey in the East that took them to Bethlehem. Jesus began a journey at Bethlehem that took him to Calvary. Our life's journey, wherever it begins and ends, will be the more purposeful if, in the words of the Epiphany hymns, we are able to say:

> All our costliest treasures bring,
> Christ, to Thee, our heavenly king.

A passage to read

Matthew 2.1–12.

A thought to ponder upon

They knelt down and paid him homage . . . opening their treasure chests, they offered him gifts of gold, frankincense and myrrh.

Jesus said, 'Where your treasure is, there your heart will be also.'

(MATTHEW 6.21)

A prayer to use

> Lord,
> help us to recognize your presence
> when you meet us in our daily life.
> Make us willing to follow the
> light you bring
> that we may find your purpose
> for our lives.

Fear in the palace

> The angel of the Lord appeared to Joseph
> in a dream and said, 'Get up, take the
> child and his mother, and flee to Egypt,
> and remain there until I tell you; for
> Herod is about to search for the child, to
> destroy him.'
>
> (MATTHEW 2.13)

There are two sides to every story. The Christmas story
is no exception. The Christian calendar makes the point.
Having celebrated the birth of our Lord on the 25 December,
the very next day we remember Stephen, martyred for his
faith in Jesus. And, within 48 hours, on the 28 December,
we are recalling to mind the slaughter of the Innocents, so
dramatically linked to the birth of that same Jesus. It seems
that Jesus, as well as bringing joy and peace, also has a dis-
turbing, even divisive effect, upon human affairs.

Mary would not have been surprised. She had been
warned to expect such contradictory reactions. Luke tells

us (2.35) that when Mary and Joseph, as the law required, presented the baby Jesus in the Temple, the aged and godly Simeon, having blessed them, went on to speak of their child's destiny. He said to Mary, 'This child is destined for the falling and rising of many in Israel, and to be a sign that will be opposed so that the inner thoughts of many will be revealed – and a sword will pierce your own soul too.' There was a price that Mary and her son must pay.

It must have been an awesome and solemn moment for the young mother. Little did she realize that opposition would come so soon. But it did, in the form of Herod who had been appointed king of the Jews by the occupying Roman authorities in 40 BC. He was a man of great ability and savage ruthlessness. There was a suspicious and cruel side to his character. He was fearful of rivals to his authority and, like so many other tyrants, his fear was expressed in violence.

The news that wise men had come to Jerusalem looking for the child who has been born king of the Jews, frightened him. Despite his great power he felt insecure. Advised by the religious leaders, he encouraged the wise men to search for the child in Bethlehem, and to let him know when and where they found him, claiming that he would also offer him homage. But, as subsequent events proved, it was homicide rather than homage he had in mind. The atmosphere in the palace of Herod the Great was anything but calm. And it got worse when the wise men, having been warned of Herod's evil intentions, took an alternative route home. Herod was furious and began to plot genocide. Mary and Joseph, being warned in a dream that Herod was going to implement a policy of search and destroy, took the child and escaped to Egypt.

They were just in time. Herod began a massacre of children of two years of age and under who lived in and around

Bethlehem. Herod's fear resulted not only in making the Holy Family refugees but also in bringing death and grief to many innocent people. This 'other side of Christmas' is not a pleasant one. It is far removed from the idyllic manger scene so often depicted on our Christmas cards. But, perhaps, it is closer to reality – too close for comfort.

After 2000 years there is still violence in God's world. Our television screens still show us thousands of refugees displaced from their homes and fleeing from the ravages of civil war. Innocent people still endure the most horrendous suffering because of the cruelty of others. Children are still the objects of abuse. Evil systems and evil people still exercise their power to destroy.

Yet Jesus came, I believe, to deliver us from evil and from fear of every kind. That is God's purpose for him, and for us. That's why Mary and Joseph, under instructions from God, took him to Egypt and later to Nazareth. He was protected from evil in the short term in order that he might confront and overcome it in the long term, as he did through the cross and resurrection.

Nevertheless, there are aspects of this side of the Christmas story that puzzle and perplex. Soft answers rarely satisfy. The slaughter of the Innocents represents the dark side of Christmas just as history reveals some of the dark things done in the name of Christianity. We can be sure of one thing, however, as the Bible makes clear, Jesus was opposed to evil wherever he found it. We must be also.

A passage to read

Matthew 2.13–23.

A thought to ponder upon

> He who passively accepts evil is as much involved in it
> as he who helps to perpetuate it.
>
> (MARTIN LUTHER KING JR, QUOTED IN
WARD AND WILD, 1997)

> Nothing else can withstand evil except the power of love.
>
> (UNA KROLL, QUOTED IN WARD AND WILD, 1997)

A prayer to use

> Lord of goodness and love
> who suffered at the hands of evil people,
> be with those who endure hurt of any kind
> and give us courage and strength to bring
> them help in their trouble.

God pitching his tent

> And the Word became flesh and lived
> among us, and we have seen his glory, the
> glory as of a father's only son, full of grace
> and truth.
>
> (JOHN 1.14)

As a bishop I always found the Midnight Eucharist in my
cathedral church very special. But my final one was unique.
Santa Claus abseiled from the tower, high above the altar,
to present me with a gift – but he never made it. I'm told
that the rehearsal earlier that day had gone like a dream but
he wasn't wearing his beard. When he wore it at midnight,
however, it got stuck in the equipment and, like the grand

old Duke of York, he found himself neither up nor down. Instead he hung suspended between heaven and earth, much to the surprise and amusement of the large congregation!

That story is absolutely true and there were at least 600 eye witnesses. Subsequently I heard four of them give their personal accounts of it. All were true and each was different. Just like the four accounts of the life of Jesus we have in the Gospels. Mark begins his story of Jesus at the River Jordan, Luke starts his with the annunciation at Nazareth, Matthew takes us back to the Old Testament and begins the story with Abraham. John, however, begins the story outside time.

He starts his account of the life of Jesus with these majestic, magnificent yet mysterious words, 'In the beginning was the Word, and the Word was with God, and the Word was God. He was in the beginning with God. All things came into being through him, and without him not one thing came into being.' The story of the babe in the manger is true. The story of the man among men, who was born as a Jew and lived at a specific time in Palestine, is true. But it is not the whole story. If you want to see the whole story it must be seen in the light of eternity. The subject of the story John tells stands beyond all time and space.

Unlike the pseudo-Santa at the midnight service, however, he was not suspended between heaven and earth. He didn't fail to make it, as it were. On the contrary, the real significance of the Christmas story is that he came to earth and, in the literal meaning of the original, 'pitched his tent' among us – 'The word became flesh and lived among us.' It is a graphic and deeply meaningful way of describing the coming of Jesus to the manger of Bethlehem and the unique life and light that he revealed to the whole world.

And it is that word 'revealed' that helps us to begin to

understand why John starts his story of Jesus by referring to him as the 'Word' (in Greek, *Logos*). There is a vast library of literature explaining the significance of this term 'Word'. To a Jew, the term Word meant the creative power of God in action. To a Greek, *Logos* also meant the rational principle behind the universe. It is through the Word that all things are created and hold together.

For our purpose it is best to go straight to the heart of the matter. The Word, or *Logos*, is the means by which God makes himself known. And, supremely, God made himself known to us not by a plan but in a person. The Word which existed before history began was clothed in flesh in the birth of Jesus, who is the revealer of God's power, wisdom and love. The God of heaven had 'pitched his tent' on earth. Heaven's life, heaven's light and heaven's love were made visible and accessible in Jesus. Small wonder that heaven's angels got so excited when Jesus was born!

John's remarkable perspective on the Child of Bethlehem is that Jesus Christ, as the Word, is the clue to all that is. He was there at the beginning of history, fully involved in creation. Born in a manger, he was the bearer of God's life, and the bearer of God's light, for 'in him was life, and the life was the light of all people'. As the eternal Word he transcends time; as the incarnate Word he divides history. This frail, vulnerable infant lying in a feeding trough is God 'pitching his tent' among us and revealing his character of generosity, faithfulness and love.

A passage to read

John 1.1–14.

A thought to ponder upon

While all things were in quiet silence, and the night was

in the midst of her swift course, thine Almighty Word, O
Lord, leaped down out of thy royal throne, alleluia.

(CHRISTMAS VESPERS: WESTERN RITE,
THE OXFORD BOOK OF PRAYER, 1985)

The *Logos* is not the exclusive property of any particular
group; on the contrary he is 'the true light that enlight-
ens everyone'.

A prayer to use

> God of grace and truth,
> may we so respond to your light
> that we receive your life
> and reflect the glory
> of the one who pitched his tent
> among us.

2

The curtain rises

In those days Jesus came from
Nazareth of Galilee and was
baptized by John in the Jordan.

(MARK 1.9)

Preparing the way

The beginning of the good news of Jesus
Christ, the Son of God. As it is written in
the prophet Isaiah, 'See, I am sending my
messenger ahead of you, who will prepare
your way; the voice of one crying in the
wilderness: "Prepare the way of the Lord,
make his paths straight."'

(MARK 1.1–3)

God is rarely, if ever, in a hurry. He is never taken by
surprise. He does his homework thoroughly, as it were, and
prepares well. Patience rather than panic characterizes his
work.

Nowhere is this better demonstrated than in those hidden,
silent years of preparation before the public ministry of
Jesus Christ began. Having chosen Mary to be the mother
of his Son, God trusted her and Joseph to fulfil the task of
guiding him through childhood and adolescence into adult
life. It wasn't all sunshine. Like every other family it had
its moments of tension, especially when he went missing
on a family outing to Jerusalem. The city was crowded for
the Passover and he was only 12 at the time. No wonder
Mary was annoyed and told him so – even though he had
been in 'church' all the time! Jesus added to the tension by
speaking of his awareness of a higher loyalty. Nevertheless,
he returned home with them and was subject to them. He
was learning that family love and loyalties have their place
and can flourish under the higher love of, and loyalty to,
God. There was no tension within God. His Son would
grow to manhood within an ordinary home. There was no
better preparation for the work he was called to do.

Eventually, God's right time arrived. And to make sure

25

that people were ready for the dramatic coming of Jesus onto the public stage he sent John the Baptist to prepare the way. It was a very special task for a very special person. Indeed, Jesus was to say of John that 'there was none greater'. He was a great prophet, a great preacher, a man of great courage and conviction and he had a great following. Thousands came out to listen to him though he didn't mince his words, calling upon people to repent and referring to some of them as a 'brood of vipers'. He challenged them to accept a radical change of lifestyle as evidence of their repentance and he left them in no doubt that judgement was just around the corner if they didn't.

John called upon people who had grown slack in their allegiance to God and complacent in their devotion to the law to 'stand up and be counted' and those who did were baptized by him in the River Jordan. It stands for ever to the credit of John that he practised what he preached. He suffered an ignominious death because he stood up for what was right in the face of shameless behaviour by King Herod. Perhaps that was the reason why John's ministry was so widely respected. People saw him as a man of integrity who not only spoke the truth but was also prepared to die for it.

As a result of John's faithful and fearless work people were filled with great expectation. For centuries devout Jewish people had been waiting for the coming of their Messiah. Such was John's influence and appeal that some felt that he was that Messiah. It was a defining moment for John. It was the precise moment for which he had been preparing. The principal player was about to make his entrance. It was time for John to leave the stage. But not before he had directed their attention to the coming one in these immortal words, 'I baptize you with water; but one who is more powerful than I is coming; I am not worthy to untie the thong of his sandals. He will baptize you with the Holy Spirit and fire.'

After that it was all uphill for John. The crowds began to desert him and follow Jesus. John's disciples were upset about this and complained. Perhaps they saw it as failure. John, however, saw it as success. It filled him with joy, the joy of the bridegroom's friend who delivers the bridegroom to the church on time and then fades into the background. This is how John put it, 'He must increase, but I must decrease.' He had fulfilled his task; he had prepared the way of the Lord.

God is not in a hurry. He doesn't cut corners or go for the 'quick fix'. He patiently pursues his purposes. They may be frustrated at times but they are always fulfilled. He invites ordinary people to share in those purposes, equips them for their task, and trusts them to do it. As time has shown, it is a winning formula. There is no greater privilege than preparing the way of the Lord.

Passages to read

Luke 2.41–52.
Mark 1.1–8.

A thought to ponder upon

> God hath sworn to lift on high
> Who sinks himself by true humility.
>
> (JOHN KEBLE, QUOTED IN
> WARD AND WILD, 1997)

A prayer to use

Lord, give me
the patience that waits trustfully on your will,

the courage that perseveres in the face of adversity,
and the humility that leads to true greatness

Identification in the water

> And just as he was coming up out of the
> water, he saw the heavens torn apart and
> the Spirit descending like a dove on him.
> And a voice came came from heaven,
> 'You are my Son, the Beloved; with you I
> am well pleased.'
>
> (MARK 1.9–11)

I vividly recall the night of my conversion to Christ. It happened quietly in my home during a week-long mission in my parish church. So by the time I got to the mission service that night I was eager and willing to respond to the general invitation of the preacher to meet with him in the church hall after the service. It was a night that changed my life. But it very nearly didn't.

My old Sunday School leader was standing guard at the door of the church hall to ensure privacy for those meeting with the missioner. He couldn't hide the surprise on his face as I approached and, to cover his embarrassment, said, 'Roy, if you want the loo, you must use another door tonight.' Recognizing the first test of my new-found commitment, I replied, 'Actually I want the Lord, not the loo.' He stood aside, puzzled that one who had been in his Sunday School and was now in the church choir, should need to meet the missioner.

But the puzzlement of my old Sunday School leader regarding one of his former pupils was as nothing compared with the astonishment experienced by John the Baptist when Jesus came to him for baptism.

John didn't have Jesus in mind when he was proclaiming a baptism of repentance to the crowds who followed him. So when Jesus asked to be baptized, John was taken aback (see also Matthew 3.13–15). It just didn't seem right. Baptism was for sinners, hence the need of repentance. Jesus was not a sinner, he didn't need to repent and, therefore, baptism was neither necessary nor appropriate. John needed to be baptized by Jesus, not the other way around.

John was embarrassed by the submission of Jesus to baptism and, for some time afterwards, so was the early Church. But Jesus knew what he was doing. He wasn't just pretending for the sake of it. It wasn't just a façade or, to use a commonplace expression, he wasn't just doing it to please his mother. It held deep significance for him. He had come into the world, 'To save his people from their sins'; and here, as a result of the preaching of John, so many of his people were aware of their need and searching for God. To Jesus, about to begin his public ministry, it was an appropriate moment to identify with those whom he had come to save. Baptism was to become of crucial importance in the life of the universal Church. Baptism matters; it mattered to Jesus; and it clearly mattered to God. No sooner had Jesus emerged from the water than God set his seal of approval on what had taken place. He did it by means of a vision and a voice.

The vision was twofold. The heavens were torn apart, and the Holy Spirit descended like a dove upon Jesus. Isaiah had prayed for the heavens to open and for God to come again as in the Exodus and deliver his people: 'O that you would tear open the heavens and come down' (Isaiah 64.1). Now, as the one who is to save or deliver his people prepares to begin his work, Isaiah's prayer is answered. And, from the open heavens, the Holy Spirit came upon Jesus in the form of a dove. The Holy Spirit was to empower him for his ministry.

But if the baptism was a means of Jesus identifying himself with sinners, it was also the occasion that God used to identify himself with Jesus. He did it not only by the vision of the divided heavens and the descending Spirit but also by the divine voice with its confirmation of the identity and authority of Jesus, 'You are my Son, the Beloved; with you I am well pleased.'

As a young Christian I was puzzled why such a humble and self-effacing person as Jesus could make such forthright claims for himself as he does in St John's Gospel. Time and again we hear him saying with authority, 'I am'; I am the light of the world, I am the way, the truth and the life, etc. I came to realize, however, that he was only able to say 'I am' with such assurance because God had first said, 'You are.'

We are whom God says we are; and God declares that in Jesus Christ we are his sons and daughters. As I discovered on that night during the mission in my parish church, 'to all who receive him, he gives power to become children of God' (John 1.12).

A passage to read

Matthew 3.13–17.

A thought to ponder upon

Christianity is about acceptance, and if God accepts me as I am, then I had better do the same.

(HUGH MONTEFIORE, QUOTED IN WARD AND WILD, 1997)

A prayer to use

> Heavenly Father,
> who at the baptism of Jesus
> revealed him to be your Son,
> anointing him with the Holy Spirit;
> help us, through that same Spirit,
> to be faithful to our calling as
> your adopted children;
> through Jesus Christ your Son our Lord.

Testing in the wilderness

> Then was Jesus led up by the Spirit into
> the wilderness to be tempted by the devil.
> He fasted forty days and forty nights, and
> afterwards he was famished.
>
> (MATTHEW 4.1–2)

We don't have to go looking for trouble. It comes looking for us. Most of us have to go through periods of conflict, tragedy and suffering. Few of us are spared those experiences of loneliness, distress and spiritual and emotional barrenness, that cause us to cry out for meaning, help and reassuring love. I have heard such things referred to as 'wilderness experiences' and, having seen the awesome barrenness, isolation and bleakness of the wilderness in Palestine, I can understand why.

Jesus was not exempt from such experiences. He was driven into the wilderness by the Spirit immediately after his baptism. The affirmation he had received in the waters of the Jordan was all too quickly replaced by the temptation in the wilderness. No sooner had his identity and authority

been established than the 'opposition' was turned loose on
him! His credentials were put to the test by the devil. And,
frankly, if he had failed the test, all the angelic activity that
surrounded his birth would have been meaningless, and
the Christian story would have ended just there – in the
wilderness. If, on the other hand, there was no possibility of
him failing the test, then the temptation was a charade,
unworthy of God and unhelpful to us.

Traditionally, the content of the three temptations has
been described as an attempt to cast doubt on his Sonship.
I am sure that is right, but I also believe there was more to
it than that. I am convinced that the temptations, whether
viewed as a literal, spiritual or psychological experience,
questioned just how that Sonship was to be expressed. The
words of the voice from heaven, 'You are my Son, the
Beloved; with you I am well pleased', were a combination of
two formulae. One was part of the coronation formula of
the kings of Israel (Psalm 2.7). The other was part of the
ordination formula of the Servant of the Lord (Isaiah 42.1).
Combined in those words from heaven, therefore, was the
concept of sovereignty and servanthood.

The subtlety of the testing in the wilderness is to cast
doubts not only on the Sonship of Jesus but also on the
manner in which that Sonship is to be exercised. The devil
suggests that the right way is the way of sovereign power.
'Command these stones to become loaves of bread.' You have
the power to do it, and it will be economically popular.
'Throw yourself down' from the pinnacle of the temple. You
are God's Son, and the Lord looks after his own; besides,
such a spectacular display is bound to win you a following.
'Fall down and worship me'; use secular methods, pick up
the sword and drive the occupying army of Rome into the
sea. That's the way to conquer the world.

On all these temptations Jesus turns his back. And in

answer to the devil's suggestions and rather selective use of Scripture, he has an appropriate response. But his threefold response to the threefold testing reveals a single and unshakeable conviction and commitment. His way would be the way of the servant. Yes, he had the authority as the Son of God, but he would win the hearts of people not by power but by service, not by force but by love.

I guess that there would have been many people in our Lord's day who would have urged him to not to resist the temptations. What's wrong with feeding the poor? What's wrong with refreshing drab lives with a bit of fun? What's wrong with using force to liberate the oppressed, wasn't Moses into that? Don't the ends justify the means? The arguments are all too familiar. 'Short termism' is the phrase used today. The temptation was an invitation to choose what was good rather than what was best.

The wilderness, however and wherever it is experienced, though difficult, is not to be despised. Sometimes that wilderness is within us. Sometimes we are surrounded by it. Loneliness, anxiety and a feeling of emptiness can be encountered anywhere. Nevertheless, the wilderness experience has so often been a prelude to and a preparation for a special piece of work for God. It was true of the Old Testament Prophets, of John the Baptist and of Jesus. And it continues to be true today for those who, in the loneliness of the wilderness experience, come face to face with God and, as a result, have their own lives transformed and make an impact on the community around them.

The time of testing is not to be despised. Some would, in hindsight, welcome it.

A passage to read

Matthew 4.1–11.

A thought to ponder upon

My child, when you come to serve the Lord, prepare
yourself for testing.

(ECCLESIASTICUS 2.1–2)

No testing has overtaken you that is not common to
everyone. God is faithful, and he will not let you be tested
beyond your strength, but with the testing he will also
provide the way out so that you may be able to endure it.

(1 CORINTHIANS 10.13)

A prayer to use

Lord,
comfort all those who
are enduring a wilderness experience, and
when it is my turn,
help me to trust in your faithfulness and loving purpose.

Standing at the gates

Now after John was arrested, Jesus came
to Galilee, proclaiming the good news of
God, and saying, 'The time is fulfilled,
and the Kingdom of God has drawn near;
repent and believe in the good news.'

(MARK 1.14–15)

Like many others who are called upon to give public
addresses, I have suffered from those who insist upon intro-
ducing me in such glowing terms as to cause me not just
acute embarrassment but a genuine anxiety lest they have
invited the wrong person. There is only one thing worse,

and that is when the one thanking you at the end gives such an inaccurate summary of what you have said or, perhaps, what he had hoped you would say, that you know they have invited the wrong person!

John the Baptist left us in no doubt that Jesus was the right person, 'Behold, here is the Lamb of God who takes away the sin of the world' (John 1.29). As for Jesus, there was no mistaking what the keynote of his faith was. It is tersely and accurately summarized, 'The time is fulfilled, the Kingdom of God has drawn near; repent and believe in the good news.'

Following his baptism in the Jordan and the temptations in the wilderness, these dramatic words marked the beginning of his public ministry in Galilee. It was a proclamation that carried an unmistakable note of urgency and climax. God's time had come. Indeed, God himself had come. The Kingdom had drawn so near that God is pictured as 'standing at the gates'.

In the light of such proximity, people are called to 'turn their minds around' and believe the good news. Repentance need not always be seen in negative terms. It is also an invitation not only to turn around but also to come and find the treasure of the Kingdom, for it is good news. The drawing near of the Kingdom was a time of opportunity. They are challenged not to miss it, but to enter and receive it.

There is no denying that in the New Testament the term, 'Kingdom of God', is a rather ambiguous one. Some saw it as belonging to the time beyond death and history, that is, something we ultimately inherit. Others referred to it as present in the ministry of Jesus; for instance in his miracles of healing. Yet others perceived it as a process which began with the coming of Jesus. There is a common factor, however, namely that in the Kingdom of God, God is King. The Kingdom of God implies the rule or reign of God.

Strangely enough a definition of the Kingdom of God is hard, if not impossible, to find in the New Testament. What Jesus meant by it can only be deduced by the things he said, the way he lived his life and the priorities he set for his ministry. There is little doubt, therefore, that the rule of God in his life was a major insight into the nature of the Kingdom – 'My food is to do the will of him who sent me and to complete his work' (John 4.34).

So also were the priorities he set in his teaching. And nowhere is this better illustrated than in his sermon on the mount in which he seemed to turn the priorities and values of society upside down, which is another characteristic of the Kingdom. The poor, the peacemakers, the hungry, the meek and the merciful are not normally listed among the top people in today's society, with its emphasis on competitiveness, strength and the survival of the fittest. How different from the Kingdom of God where, under the rule of God, such people are given priority.

Jesus taught similar truths in the stories he told. In parable after parable he gives us insight into the nature of the Kingdom by giving us insight into the nature of God. In the story of the Prodigal Son, for instance, it is the incredible generosity of God that is being emphasized (Luke 15). In the story of the Pharisee and the Publican, it is the wonderful mercy of God that is the primary characteristic of the Kingdom (Luke 18.9–14). The manner in which Jesus reached out to the poor and the outcast was a demonstration of the nature of the Kingdom, in which those who are shut out from society are brought in and welcomed.

When we pray 'your kingdom come on earth as it is in heaven', I wonder what we expect to happen? Are we thinking only of some future or distant event, or are we prepared to become part of the answer to our own prayer here and now? While not forgetting the former I believe we are committed to the latter. When, for instance, we oppose injustice, rebuke racism, combat ignorance and bring about healing and reconciliation, then the Kingdom comes and the characteristics of the rule of God are plain for all to see. The King no longer stands at the gates but enters into, and influences for good, the life of our community.

A passage to read

> Matthew 5.1–16.

A thought to ponder

> The Church is a sign of the Kingdom. It is not in the world for its own sake but for the salvation of the world.

A prayer to use

> Sovereign God,
> through our lives and by our prayers
> may your kingdom come.

Choosing the team

> And he appointed twelve, whom he also
> named apostles, to be with him, and to be
> sent out to proclaim the message, and to
> have authority to cast out demons
>
> (MARK 3.14–15)

Job interviews are becoming more and more sophisticated. All kinds of psychometric tests are now applied and, together with your Myers-Briggs Type Indicator, may determine whether or not you will get the job. Great emphasis is placed, quite rightly, not only on your ability to do the job but also on your skill in choosing and training others. The appointment of leaders who are not up to the task can spell disaster to the company in question and result in widespread redundancy. It is a serious business.

So also was the business of choosing disciples. Compared to modern-day practice, however, the methods of Jesus in choosing his team were anything but sophisticated. There were times when the kind of insights into personal temperaments as supplied by Myers-Briggs (a popular method of discovering our personality types and the preferences that emerge from them) would have helped the team to understand some of their own feelings and frustrations. Nevertheless, the founding of a world-wide Church which continues to grow, especially in the southern hemisphere, is an indication that his methods, though unsophisticated, were not unsuccessful.

Some would consider those methods somewhat akin to the modern practice of 'head hunting'. Peter and Andrew, James and John didn't apply or volunteer for the job. They were called, indeed, they were summoned, 'Follow me, and I will make you fish for people.' Four ordinary people engaged in routine activities heard the call of Jesus, left what they were doing and who they were with, and followed him.

Of course, Jesus doesn't call everyone to abandon their former occupation or relinquish their settled way of life. He must have preached to thousands without asking them to give up their work and leave home. Indeed, he expressly forbade some of those he had cured to follow him. Instead he sent them back to their domestic responsibilities. But the specific call of these first disciples is a reminder to all of us that nobody can enter the Kingdom of God without being so dedicated to God where we are – that we are ready to go anywhere and part with anything in order to follow him. That, I believe, is what Jesus meant when later in his story he said, 'If any want to become my followers, let them deny themselves and take up their cross and follow me' (Mark 8.34).

Clearly, to be a member of the Jesus team was not a sinecure, yet, today, his followers are to be numbered in hundreds of millions. But it all began with a few. Starting with the preliminary call of the four fishermen by the Sea of Galilee, it reached a seminal point with the choice and appointment of the 12 men who were to become his apostles. It was a bold move and, since one would betray him, another deny him and, at one stage, all would forsake him, somewhat risky. But he had taken a lot of care over choosing his team and had spent the night before praying about it (Luke 6.20). His judgement proved to be sound.

He was a good team leader. First, he called them to be with him, for they had much to learn. Then he gave them a task, sending them out to preach, to deliver the message they had been taught. Finally, he gave them authority to cast out demons. They were to be practitioners as well as preachers. The good news was to be in deed as well as in word.

They had their ups and downs, their failures and successes. They constantly needed reassurance. When the time came for him to leave them they panicked at the thought of carrying responsibility without the strength of his presence. However, like all good leaders, he took care of his team. They were given the gift and power of his Holy Spirit, not to make up for his absence but to intensify his presence. For they discovered as they went about their task of spreading the good news, that Jesus seemed closer to them than ever.

It is a measure of his confidence in those he had chosen that Jesus didn't have a plan 'B' up his sleeve if they had failed. It seemed an almighty and unnecessary risk to involve a bunch of fairly insignificant people in his plan to bring deliverance and wholeness to his world. But then, by any rational standards, Jesus himself was insignificant and chose a pathway that appeared foolish and ended up in failure. History has revealed, however, that God's foolishness is wiser than human wisdom, and God's weakness is stronger than human strength (1 Corinthians 1.25).

Passages to read

Matthew 4.18–22.
1 Corinthians 1.20–31.

A thought to ponder upon

Our authority to lead others in the faith will be governed by the integrity and reality of our own continued following of Jesus.

A prayer to use

Lord
thank you for calling me
and setting my feet on the way.
Help me to follow in your footsteps
and to be good news to all I meet.

Setting the pace

When they found him, they said to him, 'Everyone is searching for you.' He answered, 'Let us go on to the neighbouring towns, so that I may proclaim the message there also; for that is what I

came out to do.' And he went throughout
Galilee.

(MARK 1.37–9)

We did it when we were children. Many of us still do it
when the opportunity arises and no one is looking. Dropping
pebbles into ponds and watching, fascinated, as the ripples
move further and further outwards, has been an innocent
pastime for all ages.

It is an image that frequently comes to mind when I
think of the ministry of Jesus, though his sudden appearance
and work in Galilee produced what was more in the nature
of shock waves than gentle ripples. There was an explosive
energy and a punishing pace about his workload. It almost
makes me breathless just to read about it. Given that, 2000
years later, we are still feeling the reverberations, it is sometimes hard to believe that his public ministry lasted only
two and a half years.

Of course, the record we have in the Gospels is not a
moment-by-moment account of his ministry; far from it.
John tells us, 'that there are also many other things that
Jesus did; if every one of them were written down, I suppose
that the world itself could not contain the books that would
be written' (John 21.25). Enough has been written, however,
for us to see that Jesus was working to a tight schedule. He
knew his time was short and there was not a moment to
lose. John's enthusiastic overstatement simply serves to
emphasize the truth that Jesus, didn't 'hang about', but gave
himself completely and energetically to serve people and
their needs.

But if the pace of his ministry was demanding, the variety
of it was even more so. Within the space of a fairly typical
24-hour period we see him engaged in several emotional and
energy-sapping encounters. He visits a synagogue and gets
involved not only in teaching but also in a confrontation

with evil spirits. He pays a call at the home of Peter and Andrew and finds himself partaking in a healing service, curing Peter's mother-in-law of a fever. Supper followed, but it wasn't the prelude to an early night. On the contrary, after sunset, 'the whole city gathered around the door of Peter's house'. They had brought their sick for healing.

Whatever time he fell into bed that night he had a very early start the next morning. He rose before dawn and went out to a lonely place for a bit of peace and quiet and for prayer. But even there he was interrupted by his friends. 'Everyone is searching for you,' they said. Exactly! That is why he had come out to be alone and to pray. His popularity in that locality was such that he could easily have become bogged down with the increasing demands made upon him. But his ministry was needed not just in Capernaum but also in neighbouring towns throughout Galilee. 'Let us go there,' he said, 'for that is what I came out to do.' He knew himself to be sent by God for a specific task and that included a wider ministry of preaching and healing across Galilee. So on he went, stopping to heal a leper on the way.

Jesus was a busy person. But there seems to have been a purposefulness about his busyness. Some might look at his tight schedule and come to the conviction that, 'If a busy man like Jesus found time to pray, so should we.' I think the example of Jesus in making time to pray is more profound than that. I believe that it was because Jesus made time to pray that his busyness had such a purposefulness and power about it. It may also explain why, despite his workload, he always seemed to have time for people and, even though surrounded by crowds, was able to spot the individual who needed his help most.

We live in a competitive age where enormous pressures are placed upon those charged with leadership and responsibility, not only in society but also in the Church. Such people need our understanding and our prayers. And, if we feel ourselves to be among them, the example of Jesus is worth following. Building a space for quiet reflection and prayer into the busiest life can give it a creative and rewarding purposefulness. It may only be a few minutes that we set aside daily, or from time to time. No matter, let us learn the lesson of the pebble in the pond. The ripples spread outward until the whole pond, however gently, feels the influence of the pebble.

A passage to read

Mark 1.21–45.

A thought to ponder upon

Never say that you have no time. On the whole it is those who are busiest who can make time for yet more, and those who have more leisure-time who refuse to do something when one asks. What we lack is not time, but heart.

(HENRI BOULARD, QUOTED IN
WARD AND WILD, 1997)

A prayer to use

Lord,
in the midst of all the demands of life,
give us the heart and will to find quietness
in your presence,
that we may glimpse your glory
and be renewed in your purposes for us.

3

The plot thickens

Then he said to them all, 'If any want
to become my followers, let them deny
themselves and take up their cross daily
and follow me. For those who want to
save their life will lose it, and those who
lose their life for my sake will save it.'

(LUKE 9.23–4)

Challenging prejudice

> When he came to Nazareth, where he had
> been brought up, he went to the synagogue
> on the sabbath day, as was his custom.
>
> (LUKE 4.16–30)

Sermons are often boring; sometimes they are interesting; occasionally they are gripping. Rarely, if ever, are they life-threatening. The first recorded sermon of Jesus in his home synagogue at Nazareth was the exception to the rule, it almost cost him his life.

Ought he to have known better than upset his home congregation, especially when he was aware that 'no prophet is accepted in the prophet's own town'? Jesus knew exactly what he was doing. Challenging prejudice went with the territory.

It all started so well. 'Local boy makes good' could well have been a headline in the *Nazareth Gazette* the next morning. But it was not to be. When the time came for the reading of Scripture in the synagogue service, he unrolled the scroll and read a purple passage from the prophet Isaiah:

> The Spirit of the Lord is upon me,
>   because he has anointed me
>   to bring good news to the poor.
> He has sent me to proclaim release to the captives
>   and recovery of sight to the blind,
>   and to let the oppressed go free,
> to proclaim the year of the Lord's favour.

It had all the feel of a personal manifesto and, as events proved, it was an accurate description of the work he had come to do, namely, reverse the destiny of the poor. So, when he had handed back the scroll, sat down, and the eyes of the whole congregation were fixed on him, he said, 'Today this scripture has been fulfilled in your hearing.'

They were impressed, very impressed. There was unanimous appreciation coupled with an astonishment at the gracious words he spoke. Then it all began to go wrong. Prejudice suddenly raised its ugly head and a simple question spoke volumes, 'Is not this Joseph's son'? They began to rationalize. His words are wonderful but he is, after all, only the carpenter's son. Immediately we sense a change in the atmosphere and so did Jesus. He shows an uncanny awareness of what is going on in their minds and, taking the words from their mouths, announces what they are going to say. At that point the balloon really did go up. What on earth was going on?

His statement that, 'today this scripture is fulfilled in your hearing', had clearly fanned the flame of their expectations. But disappointment followed. It began to dawn on them that he had not read the whole of the passage from Isaiah. He had omitted the bits that spoke of the reversal of Israel's fortunes on their return from captivity. And had left out those other bits that were hostile to the Gentiles and which spoke of God getting even with them. His words about Scripture being fulfilled led them, metaphorically speaking, to expect blood on the carpet – but it hadn't materialized.

That was bad enough. But to make matters worse, he not only omits any reference to judgement on their enemies, he actually reminds them of God's compassion on those same enemies. He spoke not of God's vengeance but of his mercy shown towards a Gentile widow in Sidon and Naaman the Syrian, a Gentile leper. The congregation could not contain its fury. During the course of one sermon, admiration had turned to doubt, to anger and, finally, to attempted murder. They rushed him out of the synagogue to the brow of the hill, not a great distance in Nazareth, intending to hurl him off the cliff. However, his hour had not yet come and he escaped from their clutches and continued on his way.

I suppose Jesus could have avoided all this aggravation by not challenging their prejudices. But truth would have been the casualty of such reticence; it is always the case. In our world, within our own society and, indeed, within the Church, prejudice is all too often at the heart of conflict and controversy. Prejudice masquerading as principle prevents the truth being heard and embraced. It promotes stereotyping which can lead to intolerance and, in extreme situations, even to murder. Wherever it is found it needs to be challenged – whatever the cost.

Passages to read

Luke 4.16–30.
Isaiah 61.

A thought to ponder upon

The greatest friend of Truth is Time, her greatest enemy is Prejudice, and her constant companion is Humility.

(CHARLES CALEB COLTON, QUOTED IN
WARD AND WILD, 1997)

A prayer to use

Lord,
give me courage to challenge prejudice
within myself
that I may grow in truth and humility.

47

Words and deeds

Jesus went about all the cities and villages, teaching in their synagogues, and proclaiming the good news of the kingdom, and curing every disease and every sickness.

(MATTHEW 9.35)

Like many other doting parents I have not been averse to offering my children 'sound' advice. So, as my younger daughter prepared for an important job interview, I imparted one of my pearls of dubious wisdom. 'Dress carefully and well. If you look nice, you will be halfway there.' She was too well mannered to say, 'What a load of rubbish.' Instead, with a twinkle in her eye, she replied, 'Dad, being nice isn't good enough. I've got to be able to do the job.'

She was absolutely right, of course, as the itinerant ministry of Jesus of Nazareth so clearly demonstrated. He was immensely popular with ordinary people. They followed him in their thousands, 'listening to him with great delight'. But the secret of his popularity was not that he was 'that nice man from Nazareth' but that he delivered the goods. He was able to do the job.

The people were delighted to listen to him because he was on their wavelength. He told simple, wonderful stories using illustrations from ordinary domestic life that opened up windows into the character of God. He spoke with an authority which all recognized, though his enemies felt threatened by it. He was not concerned about making a name for himself nor, indeed, about developing a distinctive lifestyle. He pointed to God and showed the way with such integrity that he was able to say with conviction, 'Whoever has seen me has seen the Father.'

The same was true of his deeds. People were astonished by them and many had their lives radically changed as a

48

result. While John the Baptist was in prison he sent one of his disciples to Jesus to ask a rather plaintive question, 'Are you the one we were expecting or should we be looking for someone else?' The answer Jesus gave was in terms of evidence regarding his ability to do the job he had been sent to do: 'Go and tell John what you hear and see: the blind receive their sight, the lame walk, the lepers are cleansed, the deaf hear, the dead are raised, and the poor have the good news brought to them.'

It was a catalogue of competence. More than that, however, it was a demonstration of the compassionate character of God and of his ultimate purposes for humankind and the whole of his creation. When Jesus first appeared in Galilee he announced that the Kingdom of God had drawn near. The rule of God would be seen in their midst as Jesus moved through the cities and villages preaching the good news and healing the sick. Through the words and works of Jesus we are given an insight into the nature of God's Kingdom where those previously ostracized are brought in, welcomed and valued. As we follow in the footsteps of Jesus around the cities and villages of Galilee, we discover that the good news he brought consisted of words and deeds.

Good news for the blind was not just that he was the light of the world but that he removed their blindness. Good news for the lame was not just that their sins were forgiven but that he gave them power to rise up and walk. As for those with skin diseases like leprosy, good news was not only the removal of every blemish from their skin but also the removal of the ritual barrier to participation in the worshipping community. Unblocking the ears of the deaf meant they could not only hear the good news but also be included in social intercourse. Ask the widow of Nain what constituted good news for her and she would point not only to the raising of her son from the dead, but also to the fact that Jesus sent him back home to her. He was so grateful he wanted to follow Jesus. Jesus was so sensitive to the needs of his mother that he sent him packing. Holiness doesn't flourish on neglected family responsibilities. She needed his help more than Jesus needed his companionship.

A central feature of the story of Jesus is the manner in which he healed those who were said to be possessed by demons. Whatever the precise nature of the illness in question, in the eyes of Jesus and his disciples it was indicative of a deeper conflict taking place between darkness and light, between God and Satan. The exorcisms, the deliverance of the possessed person, were seen as Christ's victory over the powers of darkness. It was also a sign of the coming of the Kingdom among them, 'If it is by the finger of God that I cast out demons, then the Kingdom of God has come to you.'

We will search the Jesus story in vain for evidence that in his healing deeds he was simply showing off, misusing his power, trying to win popular support, or even prove that he was divine. On the contrary, they were an integral part of his entire ministry. His words and deeds were a seamless robe. They conveyed a single message: in Jesus, the Kingdom of God had come among us.

Passages to read

Luke 5.12–26.
Luke 7.11–23.
Luke 11.14–26.

A thought to ponder upon

Holiness doesn't flourish on neglected family responsibilities.

A prayer to use

Lord,
by the grace of your love

let our words be chosen with care and
our deeds be done with compassion;
that we may heal and not hurt
and bring comfort rather than distress.

Stand up and be counted

Then he began to teach them that the Son
of Man must undergo great suffering, and
be rejected by the elders, the chief priests,
and the scribes, and be killed, and after
three days rise again

(MARK 8.31)

One of the most enduring memories of my boyhood years is
of the day I stood at a famous meeting of waters at an Irish
beauty spot and watched, enthralled, as they flowed into
separate rivers. I found the experience awesome. It wasn't
until much later in life that I heard such a spot described as
a watershed. I was particularly interested, therefore, when I
first heard Caesarea Philippi referred to as a watershed for
both Jesus and his disciples. It is an accurate description.

Caesarea Philippi, built at the source of the River Jordan
and at the foot of Mount Hermon, marks a major division
in the story of Jesus. Up until this point, in Mark's account
of the story, Jesus had largely directed his teaching and
healing ministry towards the crowds. From this point
onward he addressed his teaching to the disciples.

There was a sense of urgency in the air. Over the weeks,
despite the wonder of his words and works, and sometimes
because of them, tensions had been developing. There were
tensions with the Pharisees about who he was and they were
forever questioning his credentials. There were tensions
with his disciples at their continuing lack of understanding

as to what he had come to do. Perhaps there were also tensions in his own mind as both these factors reminded him of the loneliness of his unique task.

The time had come for re-appraisal. The moment had arrived for him to underline the fundamental nature of his mission. Caesarea Philippi became the defining moment. The public ministry in Galilee was essentially finished. From this moment onwards the action is directed towards Jerusalem. He was on his way to Calvary.

It was time for him to assess where his disciples had reached in their understanding. So he put a preliminary question to them, 'Who do people say that I am?' Their answer revealed that he was held in high regard, but opinion was divided as to who he was. Some said, Elijah; others, John the Baptist; and still others, one of the prophets. Then came the crunch question – 'But who do you say that I am?' Peter, answered for them all and replied, 'You are the Messiah.'

It was a significant confession which, in Matthew's account, earned a special blessing from Jesus. Nevertheless it was followed immediately by a warning not to tell others. That was not as strange as it sounded. Peter and the other disciples had a growing conviction about who he was but they were still confused and uncertain about what he had come to do. They had not yet got the full picture. It was too soon to tell people who this peasant carpenter from Nazareth really was; indeed, it would have been counter-productive to have done so.

The popular image of the Messiah was that he would bring deliverance to the people of God in a spectacular manner and, perhaps, even drive the Roman army of occupation into the sea. A suffering Messiah, and one who, ultimately, would be executed as a common criminal, was anathema to the religious authorities of his day. It didn't do much for Peter's peace of mind either. He found the idea preposterous and told Jesus so, earning himself a sharp rebuke for his trouble. He and the other disciples were still blind to the nature of his Messiahship.

So Jesus began to remove their blindness by giving them a glimpse of what was to come. And, in revealing the self-giving nature of his Messiahship, he also unpacked the self-denying demands of their discipleship. It was the time to stand up and be counted. The thrill and excitement of being alongside him as he fed the multitudes, healed the sick, cast out demons and preached to popular acclaim, were soon to be replaced by confusion and despair as they journeyed with him towards his destiny of rejection and death.

Jesus left them in no doubt as to the level of commitment required of those who followed him. They too would have a cross to take up and carry. And he didn't mean poor exam results, a touch of arthritis, or an unhappy marriage. The clue to what he meant is contained in that word 'take'. It means a way of life voluntarily entered into and which involves self-denial in the service of God. Those who left their villages carrying crosses had no return ticket. They were on the way to execution.

Those who would follow Christ must leave self behind though, paradoxically, in doing so we will find our true selves. 'For those who want to save their life will lose it, and those who lose their life for my sake and the gospel, will save it.'

Passages to read

Mark 8.27–38.
Luke 9.18–27.

A thought to ponder upon

What does it profit them if they gain the whole world, but lose or forfeit themselves?

A prayer to use

> When I survey the wondrous cross
> On which the prince of glory died
> My richest gain I count but loss
> And pour contempt on all my pride.
>
> (ISAAC WATTS, 1707, ANGLICAN
HYMN BOOK)

Conflict with authorities

> The Pharisees went out and immediately
> conspired with the Herodians against
> him, how to destroy him.
>
> (MARK 3.6)

It is said, with some justification, that conflict rather than consensus sells newspapers and vastly improves the audience figures of TV programmes. If that is true, then the media, if there had been such a thing at the time of our Lord, would have had a field day. I dare say his works of mercy would have had a mention on page six of the *Jerusalem Chronicle* but the headline on page one would have doubled the circulation, 'Lay preacher in blazing row with religious authorities. Peasant carpenter takes on the Establishment.'

We don't know, of course, how Jesus would have dealt with such media coverage but we do know that he never compromised his principles in order to avoid conflict with the powers that be. And, when it came to criticism, there is evidence that he gave as good as he got. The verbal attack he launched against his opponents, including the Pharisees, was truly devastating.

> Woe to you Pharisees! For you tithe mint and rue and
> herbs of all kinds, and neglect justice and the love of God.
> Woe to you Pharisees! For you love to have

the seat of honour in the synagogues and to be greeted with respect in the market-places.

Woe also to you lawyers! For you load people with burdens hard to bear, and you yourselves do not lift a finger to ease them.

(LUKE 11.42, 43, 46)

It all seems so different from the mythical, 'Gentle Jesus meek and mild', and with good reason. The carping criticisms of those in authority, like the Pharisees, scribes and lawyers, usually arose from a situation where Jesus had done some act of love and brought help and healing to someone in need. The critics rarely had anything encouraging or compassionate to say to the one who had been healed. Instead, they dragged up some dubious point of law or tradition to question, criticize or rebuke Jesus for daring to do such a thing. In their minds, ritual was more important than reality, the traditions of the elders took precedence over the needs of the sick. They rarely missed an opportunity to undermine the person and work of Jesus.

They found fault with the company he kept, for instance, questioning the propriety of sharing a meal with tax collectors and sinners and, as so often happens with unprincipled critics, they resorted to exaggeration. Not content with calling him the friend of sinners, they dubbed him a glutton and a drunkard.

They found fault with his sabbath observance or, perhaps, his lack of it. He appeared to condone the behaviour of his disciples as they plucked ears of corn while walking through the fields. The fact that they might have been hungry mattered little. It amounted to work in the eyes of his opponents, and that was forbidden on the sabbath. So also was his healing of a man with a withered hand in the synagogue. As far as his critics were concerned, such action infringed the law even if it did deliver a person from distress.

Jesus, however, refused to ignore such a legalistic attitude. He challenged them, 'Is it lawful to do good or to do harm on the sabbath, to save life or to destroy it?' They couldn't give him a sensible answer. They sat in silence and seethed with anger. On another occasion in similar circumstances he put his finger very firmly on a sore spot as he said to them, 'If one of you has a child or an ox that has fallen into a well, will you not immediately pull it out on a sabbath day?' His reasoning was beyond question. Wisely, they kept quiet.

But he wouldn't let them off the hook. There was too much at stake. He spelt out a basic principle of creation, namely, that 'The sabbath was made for humankind and not humankind for the sabbath.' In other words the laws of sabbath observance were there to serve people. Their purpose was not to impose burdens but to bring renewal of life and to help them to be the sort of people God intended.

It was a theme he returned to again and again as his opponents kept up a running battle on one subject after another. It was vitally important that he challenged their criticisms which, so often, were founded on the traditions of men rather than the ways of God. If he had failed to do so, the good news that he came to bring would have been distorted if not destroyed. The One he had come to reveal was not a God of rule and regulation but a God of grace and compassion. He had come not to build ritual barriers but to open doors of welcome into the Kingdom of God.

Passages to read

Mark 2.13 — 3.6.
Luke 11.37–53.

A thought to ponder upon

You are a poor soldier of Christ if you think that you can

overcome without fighting, and suppose that you can have the crown without the conflict.

(JOHN CHRYSOSTOM, CHURCH FATHER, QUOTED IN
WARD AND WILD, 1997)

A prayer to use

> God of grace and compassion,
> give me courage to confront injustice
> and all that would seek to diminish
> your good news of life and freedom.

Glory on the mountain

> Now about eight days after these sayings
> Jesus took with him Peter and John and
> James, and went up on the mountain to
> pray.
>
> (LUKE 9.28)

At the summit of Mount Tabor, in the land of Galilee, stands a beautiful church building commemorating the transfiguration of our Lord. I have worshipped there on three occasions but, strangely, I remember it not so much for the sense of the mysterious within the building itself but because of the terrifying experience of getting there.

A firm of Bedouin taxi drivers seems to have a monopoly on getting people to the church on time. With only inches to spare between their wheels and a sheer drop into the valley, they drive stretch-limos at breakneck speed round hairpin bends while answering mobile phones and, at the top, disgorge passengers whose fear of God has increased sharply on the way. It is no comfort to realize that it is even more hair-raising on the way down. Nevertheless the journey is worth it. To visit the Mount of Transfiguration is a memorable, awe-inspiring experience.

Certainly, Peter, James and John must have found it so. Indeed, I would not be at all surprised to learn that at one point in the proceedings the hairs stood out on the back of their neck. The dazzling brightness, the historical visitors, the enveloping cloud and the voice must have sent their nerves tingling. I don't think even Bedouin taxi drivers could have produced a dramatic effect like that.

But it wasn't just the setting that was significant, it was the timing. The story begins, 'Now eight days after these sayings.' What sayings? The sayings at Ceasarea Philippi about who Jesus was and what he had come to do. The experience at Caesarea Philippi was shattering for Peter and the other disciples. The revelation by Jesus that he would be rejected and killed, and the whole emphasis on self-denial, suffering and death, must have left them depressed and very uncertain. They had forsaken all to follow one they believed to be the Messiah. Now, apparently, it was all going to end in tragedy. Even his mention of rising again the third day hadn't registered. The thought of his public execution didn't inspire hope for the future.

So Jesus, eight days later, provides them with an experience that puts the gloom of Caesarea Philippi into perspective – the perspective of glory. He invited the three leading disciples to go with him as he went up the mountain to pray. As he prayed he was transfigured, his countenance and his clothes enveloped in a dazzling light symbolizing the glory of God. In the midst of this brightness he is joined by Moses and Elijah, representing the law and the prophets. The topic of their conversation, according to Luke, is his departure or exodus. In other words they were discussing his forthcoming death.

The significance of this discussion is that the topic

which had caused the disciples such alarm and despondency at Ceasarea Philippi is now being considered within the context of glory – the glory of God. Far from his death being a disaster, it was the will of God which, in love, he had chosen to obey. Perfect, self-giving love between Father and Son is the essence of glory. It was an awesome moment and the disciples didn't want to let go of it. Peter, with typically thoughtless enthusiasm, offered to mark the time and place for posterity. While he was speaking, however, a cloud over-shadowed them and they were terrified because it was a further powerful indication of the presence of God with them. And, sure enough, the voice of God came from the cloud, 'This is my Son, my Chosen; listen to him.' In other words, they must heed what they had heard from him at Caesarea Philippi.

So, here in the midst of the vision on the mountain, just as in the water of the Jordan, the identity of Jesus was reinforced and, in a most dramatic way, the nature of his Sonship was endorsed. Suffering and death do not lie as an impassable obstacle across the way. On the contrary, they are on the way; indeed, they open up the way to the completion of God's purposes.

All too quickly, perhaps, we are tempted to look for the immediate application of this story to life today. All too readily we draw comparisons with our own so-called mountaintop experiences. That is natural and it may be right. But we must not ignore the mystery that surrounds the transfiguration of Jesus. The disciples who were present didn't grasp its full significance at the time. The frightening presence of God seemed to reduce them to silence, for they didn't speak about it with understanding until much later. After the resurrection the pieces of the jigsaw began to fit together and they were able to speak of the transfiguration as good news.

On the mountain of transfiguration the subject was

death – death within the context of God's glory. That must be its true relevance in every age, namely, that carried into the larger context of the glory of God, supremely displayed in cross and resurrection, all things, including death, are transfigured.

Passages to read

Mark 9.2–13.
Luke 9.28–36.

A thought to ponder upon

I've been to the mountain top. And I've looked over, and I have seen the promised land . . . I'm not fearing any man. Mine eyes have seen the glory of the coming of the Lord.

(MARTIN LUTHER KING JR, QUOTED IN WARD AND WILD, 1997)

A prayer to use

Lord,
give us glimpses of your glory
as we follow in your footsteps
day by day.

Failure in the valley

When he had entered the house, his disciples asked him privately, 'Why could we not cast it out?' He said to them, 'This kind can come out only through prayer.'

(MARK 1.28–9)

It seems to be part of the rhythm of life that after a period of jubilation there follows soon afterwards a contrasting experience of despondency or despair. I vividly recall, for instance, returning from wonderful family holidays and, as we got close to my vicarage, whispering to my wife lest the children should hear, 'I wonder what disaster is waiting for us this time?' It wasn't the comment of a cynic but of a realist. It had happened so often before that, in a strange way, I was looking forward to it.

Perhaps it was an acknowledgement of this aspect of human life that prompted the writers of the first three Gospel records to place the story of the demon-possessed boy immediately after the transfiguration. There couldn't have been a greater contrast between the scene Jesus left on the mountain and that which awaited him in the valley below. Glory gave way to gloom. Jubilation was replaced by despair. The three disciples on the mountain tried to retain the wonder of their experience. Those in the valley wished to forget theirs as soon as possible. It was disappointing and distressing for all concerned.

The boy's father was disappointed. In faith he had brought his son to Jesus for healing and he wasn't there. So he placed his trust in the disciples and they failed to deliver. The boy remained in the distressing condition, which some describe as epilepsy, that had afflicted him from childhood. The disciples were disappointed. They fully expected to be able to heal the lad after all, they had done this sort of thing before. But they failed miserably and, perhaps, much to the delight of the disputing scribes who may have welcomed the opportunity to embarrass Jesus. Jesus himself was disappointed not only that the boy remained afflicted but also that his disciples had been found wanting. The father's faith had been rewarded by failure.

Jesus addressed strong words to the crowd, including the disciples, about their faithlessness and then got a grip of the situation. He asked for the boy to be brought to him and invited the father to disclose a little of his case history. The father, clearly at his wit's end, finished his account with the desperate plea, 'If you are able to do anything, have pity on us and help us.'

The response of Jesus was swift and unexpected, 'If you are able! – All things can be done for the one who believes.' Jesus, therefore, throws the onus back on to the father by saying that a person who has faith will not set limits on what Jesus or God can do. That certainly seems to be how the father understands the meaning of the reply from Jesus. He saw it as a gentle rebuke and a clear challenge regarding his faith. His response was memorable, 'I believe; help my unbelief.'

But it was also a model response, full of integrity. He did have a measure of faith, otherwise he wouldn't have come looking for Jesus in the first place. He did so want his son to be set free from affliction and, I guess, was prepared to do anything to make it happen. However, he knew his own shortcomings in this matter of faith and wasn't prepared to promise more than he could honestly deliver. He asked, therefore, for help where his faith fell short. It was immediately forthcoming. No disappointment this time. His son was delivered from his affliction.

Then came the post mortem. 'Why could we not cast it out?' asked the disciples. 'This kind can come out only through prayer,' he replied, thus giving the clue to their failure. Jesus wasn't implying that if they prayed more they would have greater success in the future. It wasn't a plea for increased piety. Rather, it was a call to return to that point from which all true prayer springs, namely, complete dependence on God. I think there is a hidden warning in our Lord's words not to take God for granted.

When Jesus had sent them out round the villages (Mark 6.1–12) he gave them authority to cast out demons and they had done so. Perhaps they thought the authority given then, was now theirs and they could exercise it as they chose without reference to Jesus. But God doesn't put his power under the control of people in that kind of way, to dispose of it as they see fit. There is always a need for us to ask for it and to receive it for what it is, a gift from God.

'Bring him to me' were the words that transformed the situation in the valley. Once the boy was brought to the source of healing and wholeness he was delivered from his affliction and the glory of God was seen in the valley just as it had been seen on the mountaintop.

A passage to read

Mark 9.14–29.

A thought to ponder upon

You have gone up into the mountain of sacrifice, while I still dwell in the valley of care, and have spent almost all my life for others.

You take the wings of contemplation and soar above all this, but I am so stuck in the glue of concern for other people that I cannot fly.

(PETER MARTYR, ITALIAN DOMINICAN FRIAR, QUOTED IN
WARD AND WILD, 1997)

A prayer to use

Lord,
You are the God of the mountaintop
    and the God of the valley.
When success comes my way,
    give me grace to thank you.
When failure looks me in the face,
    help me to trust you.

4

The climax approaches

Thomas, who was also called the Twin,
said to his fellow disciples, 'Let us also
go up to Jerusalem, that we may die with him.'

(JOHN 11.16)

Action replay

> As he came near and saw the city, he
> wept over it, saying, 'If you, even you, had
> only recognized on this day the things
> that make for peace! But now they are
> hidden from your eyes.'
>
> (LUKE 19.41–2)

Those who watch sport on TV are familiar with the term
action replay. A goal is scored, a wicket is taken, a trophy is
won and the magic moment is not only caught on screen,
it is played over and over again for our enjoyment.
Sometimes, it has to be said, the action is repeated so often,
and from so many angles, that we end up being bored to
tears – especially if the action in question has been against
our particular team.

Though I have never heard them described as such, the
events of Palm Sunday, which began the last week of our
Lord's earthly life, have always seemed to me to have
the nature of an action replay of his temptation in the
wilderness (Matthew 4.1–11). As he stood on the hill over-
looking the Holy City, he must have seen all the elements
of the wilderness temptations. The stones, the crowds, the
Temple, the soldiers, together with those plotting his down-
fall, were all there.

The essence of the temptations had been the winning of
popular support by dubious means. So you are the Son of God
whose task is to win the world for God – here is how you do
it. Turn stones into bread. Give the crowds a spectacular
display by leaping off the Temple pinnacle. Use force to
liberate the people and drive the occupying Roman soldiers
into the sea. Now, here he was, looking across at the
Temple, surrounded by crowds, including soldiers and, as
always in Jerusalem, stones were within easy reach.

It must have been a poignant moment, as he recollected the temptation to win the approval of the crowds, to be surrounded by multitudes who sang his praise, spread palm branches in his path and cried, 'Hosanna, to the Son of David! Blessed is the one who comes in the name of the Lord! Hosanna in the highest heaven!'

It is worthy of note that Jesus accepted their welcome gladly and without cynicism – though he must have known of the sinister secular and religious powers that would unscrupulously manipulate the situation for their own ends. All too soon voices raised in praise would be replaced by those raised in condemnation. Cries of 'hosanna' would all too easily become screams of 'crucify'. But just as he was not deflected by the subtleties of Satan's temptations so he was not deluded by the welcome and popular acclaim of the Palm Sunday multitude. He received their God-given praise and told those who wished to shut them up that if they did so the stones would cry out in praise.

As for the Temple, he must, like any other Jewish man, have been been thrilled at the sight of this sacred place, so significant in the history of the people of God. However, far from casting himself down from its pinnacle, he goes to the heart of its tragedy and folly. What was meant to be the symbol of God's grace and glory had now become, in part, the centre of a religious sub-culture in which the human activities of buying and selling resulted in people, and particularly the poor, being excluded.

He gave the money-changers short shrift and drove them out of the Temple. He had come to bring good news to the poor – not to exclude them from it! At the end of the week, however, he found himself excluded, pushed outside the city walls to an unhallowed place and nailed to a cross. The Temple, which seemed indestructible, would soon be destroyed. Jesus, who seemed so dispensable, despised, broken and dead, would soon be raised up. He would build a new Temple made of living stones, of people made alive with his life. That living Temple would not be a place of exclusion but the place of forgiveness, healing, reconciliation and acceptance.

In the light of the action replay of Palm Sunday, how wise Jesus was to resist the wilderness temptations. How foolish he would have been to take a short cut in doing the will of God by following the way of popular acclaim. Action replays on television never vary. They always record the same thing. The same person scores the same goal. With Jesus it was different. His triumph over Satan in the wilderness proved to be but a foretaste of that greater victory that would take him and us beyond the darkness of Good Friday to the joy of Easter Day.

Passages to read

Matthew 21.1–17.
Luke 19.28–48.

A thought to ponder upon

Children wave their palms
as the King of all kings rides by;
should we forget to praise our God,
the very stones would sing.

(MIMI FARRA, *MISSION PRAISE*, 1990)

A prayer to use

Lord,
you came to your world in meekness and majesty,
help us to welcome you with humility
and to serve you as King.

Love's extravagance

> While he was at Bethany in the house of
> Simon the leper, as he sat at table, a
> woman came with an alabaster jar of very
> costly ointment of nard, and she broke
> open the jar and poured the ointment on
> his head.
>
> (MARK 14.3)

The excitement of that first Palm Sunday quickly gave way to a day of intrigue. Public praise had dominated the arrival of Jesus in Jerusalem, riding on a donkey. Private plotting took centre stage in the days that followed. His enemies did shady deals in dark corners, determined to destroy Jesus by forcing him into confrontation with the religious and civic authorities.

But in the midst of the gloom of intrigue there was a glimmer of light. Into the darkness of manipulation and deceit there shone an act of beauty and devotion that has never been forgotten, though the accounts of it vary. It happened at Bethany in the home of Simon the leper. Jesus had gone there to stay after his tiring and triumphant entry into Jerusalem. At some point during the meal a woman who was present came to Jesus and caused quite a stir. She broke open the alabaster jar of costly ointment she was carrying and poured the contents over his head.

To say that those who watched her were annoyed would be an understatement. They were furious. They saw it as a misuse of a valuable resource. They felt that the ointment would have been better sold and the proceeds given to the poor. The world has never been short of those who insist on telling us of a better way to spend our money!

But though they saw it as gross extravagance, Jesus didn't. He saw it for what it was – a generous and symbolic gift out of a loving and perceptive heart. It was in total contrast to the meanness and manipulation he would experience in Jerusalem during the rest of the week. As Archbishop Stuart Blanch has written, 'Judas was to be remembered for his treachery, Caiaphas for his cynical use of power, Pilate for his flagrant breach of justice: this unnamed woman was to be remembered throughout the world wherever the gospel was preached for her simple, spontaneous, uncalculating act of love.'

As far as this woman was concerned, her devotion towards Christ was beyond calculation. No appropriate price tag could be placed upon it. Of course, in economic terms, the spending of scarce resources on the economically unviable was not good practice. And lavishing so much on a loser doomed for extinction was a poor return for such generosity.

But there was more to it than that. When Jesus had entered Jerusalem on Palm Sunday people began recalling the Old Testament prophecy, 'Behold your king comes, riding on an ass.' But there was no coronation for this king – only crucifixion. So the woman, perhaps unwittingly, was not just performing the common courtesy towards a distinguished guest, she was doing much more. The anointing of the head was part of the ritual of the coronation service for the kings of Israel. The woman, therefore, in anointing the head of Jesus was acknowledging him as the Messiah, the true King of Israel, in whose kingdom values, including economic ones, are turned upside down.

But, as Jesus explained, there were also other depths of symbolism in her generosity. It was a preparation for his burial. She had acknowledged him as king but, with prophetic insight, knew that his crown would be a crown of thorns. She perceived what others had failed to understand that, humanly speaking, it was all going to end in tears. She saw with the eyes of faith what the leaders in Jerusalem had been too blind to see. Unlike them, she recognized the time of opportunity, and seized the chance to do what she could and express the love of her heart. The breaking of the jar of costly ointment which marked the extravagance of her love was but a reflection of the unique extravagance of God's love in the brokenness and outpouring of the life of his only Son.

There is yet more mystery in this wonderful story. The anointing at Bethany took place before his death because there would not be enough time after death to perform all the normal rites which follow death. When the women went to perform some of those rites early on Easter morning the body was gone! So this simple, yet prophetic, sign turns out to be not only a sign of Messiahship and coming death, but it is also a sign of coming resurrection.

What had been hidden from the powerful and wise was disclosed by the action of this humble woman in a village home. Thus God hides his ways from the proud but makes them known to the humble in heart.

A passage to read

Mark 14.1–9.

A thought to ponder upon

Too many have dispensed with generosity to practise charity.

(EDMUND BURKE, QUOTED IN WARD AND WILD, 1997)

A prayer to use

God our Father,
you spent yourself to the full

in the extravagant gift of your Son.
Preserve us from meanness of mind
and give us generous hearts.

Glory on the floor

During supper Jesus, knowing that the
Father had given all things into his hands,
and that he had come from God and was
going to God, got up from the table, took
off his outer garment, and tied a towel
around himself.

(JOHN 13.3–4)

It was meant to be a farewell meal. It became a drama of
enormous significance. Towels and basins are not normally
the stuff of which revolutions are made. But there's always
a first time and the Last Supper in that upper room in
Jerusalem provided it. There on the floor, before the astonished eyes of his disciples, Jesus revealed to them a revolu-
tionary idea of greatness. It was a lesson they needed to
learn and one they would never forget.

On the way to the upper room they had been arguing as
to who was the greatest among them (Luke 22.24–7). They
were, perhaps, so preoccupied with this question of precedence and status that, when they arrived for supper, they
were in no mood to perform the common courtesy of
washing the dust from one another's feet. Their surprise,
therefore, must have been all the greater when Jesus got up
from the supper table, took off his outer garment, tied a
towel around his waist and filled a basin with water. 'What
on earth is he doing?' they may have thought, 'This isn't
part of the passover ritual.'

What happened next, however, really did 'put the cat among the pigeons'. For he knelt on the floor and began to wash their feet. And they let him do it. They let him do it, that is, until he got to Peter, who would have none of it. He was incensed at the prospect. There was no way he was going to let Jesus wash his feet. 'Unless I wash you,' said Jesus, 'you have no share with me.' In response Peter opted not just for a footwash but for a bath, 'Lord, not my feet only but also my hands and my head!' Jesus assured him there was no need. The amount of water wasn't important. What it signified was what mattered; the footwashing was sufficient.

So Jesus continued to wash feet, including Peter's, and, in doing so, gave them a practical demonstration of the principle that controlled his life and ministry, namely, serving the needs of others. In their pride they had refused to do what he had been doing all his life – taking the lowest place. The scene on the floor of that upper room was a microcosm of his entire life. He came from God, creator of the universe, yet he chose to enter history as a baby in a barn. Into his hands were given all the Father's authority and power, yet he chose to lead men and women rather than drive them, using his power to serve and heal them. Metaphorically speaking, he was always scraping dirt from people's feet, dealing with their sickness and their sin.

But surely kneeling on the floor was a posture for servants, not for kings. Was that, perhaps, the thinking behind Peter's protest? Was his idea of a Messiah incompatible with kneeling on the floor washing dirty feet? He had to learn that both were completely consistent, for Jesus combined both roles. He was the Servant King whose sovereignty was exercised in costly service.

So in that upper room not only were their feet being washed but categories of thought were being exploded. The mindset of the disciples was being challenged. The foot-washing was not just a nice example of humility and service, it was much more. It was a dramatized parable of the kind of service he was offering to the world and of which he spoke as he broke the bread and poured out the wine at supper. 'This is my body. This is my blood. Given for you' (1 Corinthians 11.23–6). The bread and the wine on the table in the upper room were intimately connected with the towel and basin on the floor: they declared the same message.The glory of God is to be seen in the humiliation of the cross and in practical, loving service towards others. The cleansing of their feet on the floor was a picture of the greater cleansing and renewal he would bring them, and all humankind, through his cross.

That was the significance behind his confrontation with Peter. Unless you are prepared to receive the cleansing that I bring you through the cross, unless you let me serve you in this way, you can have no share in my life or my work.

Peter was learning that true humility does not begin with the giving of service but with the readiness to receive it. And, though he didn't realize it at the time, he was also being given a glimpse of the glory of God. At its root, glory means the outworking of character, and there on the floor an aspect of the character of God was being displayed. What is God like? He is like Jesus kneeling on the floor washing dirty feet.

A passage to read

John 13.1–20.

A thought to ponder upon

The insignia of the kingdom of God is not crowns and

coronets, but towels and basins.

(T. W. MANSON, *THE TEACHING OF JESUS*, 1931)

A prayer to use

> Servant King,
> help me to receive service
> as well as give it.

Yes

> He said, 'Abba, Father, for you all things
> are possible; remove this cup from me;
> yet, not what I want, but what you want.'

(MARK 14.36)

Anyone visiting the Holy Land cannot avoid the widespread presence of olive trees. Tour guides invariably draw attention to them and also to the ancient presses that helped to produce the oil that was so essential to life in that land.

It takes but a moment's reflection to make the connection with the term gethsemane – which means, 'press of oils' – and that garden on the Mount of Olives where Jesus was 'hard pressed' by an overwhelming experience of sorrow and desolation. It was that experience which gave the term its enduring and world-wide significance. Gethsemane describes those tragic experiences of life when we are really up against it and are victims of circumstances from which there is no escape. Nevertheless, there was something unique about the experience in the Garden of Gethsemane.

Jesus was alone. He didn't particularly want to be alone, indeed, he had brought three of his closest friends with him for support but they were weary and fell asleep. But there was no sleep for him. He was engaged in some kind of spiritual struggle or moral dilemma. One record (Luke 22.44) refers to him praying to God with such intensity that the sweat on his brow 'became like great drops of blood falling down to the ground'. His sorrow was beyond human comprehension.

Yet it was in the midst of the sorrows of Gethsemane that Jesus said his glorious 'Yes' to God in the immortal words, 'Not my will but thine be done' – 'Not what I want but what you want.' The words marked the culmination of the struggle in the garden where he had not been spared the agony of confusion and uncertainty. Jesus was truly human as well as truly God. He had a human fear of suffering and death and a divine abhorrence of sin. The agony of Gethsemane was that of the innocent recoiling from guilt, of the human will of Jesus intruding itself upon the will of God. The thought of bearing the sin of the world was crushing and overwhelming.

It was Archbishop William Temple who said of Jesus' words that, 'The Church has turned what was a battle cry into a wailing litany' and he was right. They are not meant to express 'the baffled resignation of a beaten soul' but the joyful acceptance of a better way. The prayer is not a moan but a glad 'Yes' to the will of God his Father. Nevertheless, there are mysterious elements in the agony in Gethsemane whose depths we cannot hope to reach, let alone understand. Whatever else was involved, however, we are back once more to that question which surfaced again and again throughout his ministry, namely, what Sonship meant to Jesus.

As a 12 year old he had insisted that he must be about his Father's business (Luke 2.49). At his baptism and transfiguration he had heard the voice of God lovingly refer to him as 'my Son'. So what is involved in being God's Son? The

Gethsemane prayer of Jesus speaks of two elements. The first is complete trust in the providential ordering of God – 'Abba, Father, for you all things are possible; remove this cup from me.' The second is complete obedience – 'Yet, not what I want but what you want.'

As the storm clouds of imminent crucifixion gathered around him Jesus didn't sail through this particular trial in total calmness of spirit. He was in deep distress. Was there no way out? Did he not have a choice? Were there no options? Was there not a better way? Whatever the answer to these questions may be, his struggle in Gethsemane was real and had all the signs of a moral dilemma. It was his willingness to trust and obey which made a way forward possible. The victory that the cross ultimately proved to be, was won in the prayer struggle at Gethsemane. That and that alone explains the silent dignity and the serene manner in which he endured the betrayal, insults and injuries and the ignominious end to his unique life.

Courage is said to be the basis of all virtue. Jesus had it in abundance. It was courage that helped him to admit his fear and it was courage that enabled him to say his great 'Yes' to God his Father – and so begin his final journey.

Passages to read

Mark 14.32–42.
Luke 22.39–46.

A thought to ponder upon

He went to the Garden of Gethsemane to wait upon the outcome. Waiting can be the most intense and poignant of all human experiences – the experience which, above all others, strips us of our needs, our values and ourselves.

(W. H. VANSTONE, QUOTED IN WARD AND WILD, 1997)

A prayer to use

> Lord,
> when loneliness overwhelms me
> and I am hard pressed by circumstances
>   beyond my control,
> give me courage to wait on your unfolding will
> and the strength to trust in your unfailing love.

Never say never

> Peter said to him, 'Though all become
> deserters because of you, I will never
> desert you.'
>
> (MATTHEW 26.33)

I like to listen to famous people being interviewed on television or radio, especially if they are reminiscing about their life and work. As the interview draws to a close the interviewer usually poses a final question, 'If you had to live your life all over again, would you change anything?'

I wait for the answer with bated breath because it determines, for me, the integrity of all that has gone before. If the answer is, 'No, I wouldn't change a thing,' I am disappointed and full of scepticism. It seems to imply that the interviewee had gone through life without learning a thing. If, however, the answer is something like, 'Oh, yes, there's lots I would change', I breathe a sigh of relief and feel that I'm in touch with reality.

If Peter had been interviewed towards the end of his life, there is little doubt that, with deep emotion, he would have given the second answer. And I can imagine him continuing, 'Oh, how I wish I had never said never. If only

I had kept my mouth shut. I was trying to be bold in support of my friend, Jesus. But the words came out all wrong and it sounded boastful and arrogant, and I lived to regret it.'

Peter was a great character. Never backward about coming forward. There was no doubting his love for Jesus nor his courage in the face of danger. It was Peter, for instance, who produced the sword in Gethsemane and jumped to the defence of Jesus when the soldiers came for him. Peter's heart was big but so too was his mouth – and he was forever putting his foot in it. You could always rely on Peter for a quick comment but his comments were not always reliable. There were times when he seemed to have learned nothing during his three years' companionship with Jesus. But, like the rest of us, he learnt the hard way – by his mistakes, particularly during that final week in Jerusalem.

After the Last Supper in the upper room the disciples had sung a hymn and then walked with Jesus to the Mount of Olives close by. Knowing what was in store for him that night he, with great sensitivity and understanding, tried to prepare them for it. He warned that natural fear, when faced with the danger of death, would cause them to desert him. He even accompanied the warning with a promise that all would be well eventually. But Peter wasn't listening. He was too intent on getting in with a quick word, 'Though all become deserters because of you, I will never desert you.' Boldness bordering on boastfulness.

Jesus again tried to warn him, for he knew that Peter wasn't as strong as he thought he was and, besides, it is difficult to think straight when you're scared stiff. 'Truly I tell you, this very night, before the cock crows, you will deny me three times.'

Oh dear! If only Peter had bitten his tongue at this point. It was a time for swallowing hard and saying nothing, but that wasn't Peter's way. He meant well, I am sure, but again the words came out all wrong. 'Even though I must die with you, I will not deny you.' The warning of Jesus went unheeded. Within hours Peter's vow, neither to desert nor deny Jesus, lay in tatters and he was in deep shock and despair. He had broken his promise. 'I will never desert you,' he said – but he did. 'I will never deny you,' he vowed – but he did, three times!

The desertion was bad enough, though he was not alone in such an action, for all the disciples did the same thing. It was the denial that rocked him to his very foundations. To think that he could do such a thing and in such shameful circumstances. He wasn't being tortured by soldiers at the time. He was simply responding to the observations of a quick-witted, sharp-eyed servant girl. She recognized him as belonging to Jesus and told him so. Three times over the accusation was levelled at Peter and each time he vehemently denied the truth, on the third occasion with oaths and curses.

It was a sad and shameful performance and Peter knew it for as he uttered his third denial the cock crowed and the implication of what he had done overwhelmed him. At that moment Jesus turned and looked straight at him. It was that look, whatever message it conveyed, that broke Peter's heart for 'He went outside and wept bitterly.'

In the light of what transpired after the resurrection I don't believe that the look directed by Jesus towards Peter was one of rebuke, nor was it a vengeful 'I told you so' expression. From what we know of Jesus that would have been unworthy. I believe it was a look of love and under-standing. That was enough to break anyone's heart and, of course, to suggest that his failure was not the end of the matter. There was hope beyond despair. Broken hearts can be mended.

Open Return

Passages to read

Matthew 26.30–5, 69–75.
Luke 22.54–62.

A thought to ponder upon

Christianity is not for us unless we are able to face the
fact that failure exists.

(ENOCH POWELL, QUOTED IN WARD AND WILD, 1997)

A prayer to use

Lord,
when we fail you,
in your mercy
forgive and restore us.

5

The curtain falls

The seven words of Jesus
from the Cross open up a
window into the heart of God.

Forgiveness

Jesus said, 'Father forgive them; for they
do not know what they are doing.' And
they cast lots to divide his clothing.

(LUKE 23.34)

It is significant that our Lord's first word from the cross is a
prayer. His whole life had been a prayer to his Father, for
it had been lived in obedience to the Father's will. Prayer
came naturally to him. As he hung on the cross, humanly
speaking, prayer was about the only thing left to him.
Hands which had touched and healed the sick were now
held helpless by wood and nails. No longer can his feet take
him on journeys of compassion, they are fastened to the
cross. Even if he had felt like giving his disciples a last word
of encouragement, there was no point, they had all forsaken
him and fled. So he prayed for forgiveness.

His prayer revealed that his faith in his Father is
unshaken and his love for people is undiminished. He
knows that he is innocent of the charge levelled against him.
All during the mockery of a trial he had remained passive,
refusing to swap insults or descend to the level of those
taunting him with abuse. And now on the cross, despite
the indignity and injustice of it all, there is no word of
recrimination, no call for vengeance, no bitter complaint.
Just a prayer for those who have crucified him. 'Father,
forgive them; for they do not know what they are doing.'

If, in these words, Jesus was referring to the soldiers who
nailed him to the cross, then it is true, they didn't merit
either condemnation or judgement. They were simply doing
what they had been ordered to do. If, however, he was
referring to those who through personal hatred and manipulative plots had brought about his crucifixion then, at first

83

glance, it may seem hard to justify his gracious claim of ignorance. Yet even they thought they were merely putting an end to an upstart peasant carpenter from Nazareth who insisted on blasphemy. They didn't know that they were executing the Son of God.

The prayer for forgiveness embraced all who were involved in or responsible for his crucifixion (Acts 3.17; 13.27). Jesus was simply remaining true to his own vision. God was still his Father and love for his enemies had always been his practice. So why should he change now? 'Love is patient; love is kind,' wrote St Paul (1 Corinthians 13). But where did he learn that? He learnt it not only from what others told him of these words of Jesus from the cross, but also from personal experience as he, a persecutor of Christ and his Church, discovered that he also was loved and forgiven.

Forgiveness was so important to Jesus that he made it an integral part of the special prayer he taught his disciples. 'Forgive us our sins as we forgive those who sin against us.' In other words, forgiveness is not just an occasional good-natured act. For the Christian it is meant to be an attitude of mind and, perhaps, the hidden implication of that phrase from the Lord's Prayer is that those who are forgiven must themselves become forgiving. It is by forgiving that we are forgiven.

Many of the intractable problems between people and nations can only be solved by the application of a spirit of forgiveness. But forgiveness is no easy matter. It is costly to forgive. It is sometimes costly to be forgiven. Yet, in order for it to be complete, forgiveness needs to be accepted as well as offered.

Father, forgive them; for they do not know what they are doing.

A passage to read

Luke 23.32–8.

A thought to ponder upon

He who cannot forgive others, breaks the bridge over
which he himself must pass.

(CORRIE TEN BOOM, QUOTED IN
WARD AND WILD, 1997)

A prayer to use

Lord,
forgive me and make me more forgiving.
Help me to accept forgiveness with humility
and to offer it without pride.

Promise

Then he said, 'Jesus, remember me when
you come into your kingdom.' He replied,
'Truly I tell you, today you will be with
me in Paradise.'

(LUKE 23.42–3)

Jesus was nothing if he was not consistent. He had been
criticized in life for keeping bad company with sinners and
prostitutes. Here he is, at the point of death, again in the
company of outcasts, among, as it were, the flotsam and
jetsam of the world. Isaiah had prophesied that the ideal
Servant of the Lord would be 'numbered with the trans-
gressors' (Isaiah 53.12). Having identified himself with

sinners at his baptism as he began his public ministry, so he is found in their company as that ministry draws to a close. The Son of God dies between two criminals.

And, despite his own agony of body and mind, he is forced into a three-way conversation with them. One of his companions, taking his lead from the rulers and the soldiers, also decides to have a go at Jesus. 'Are you not the Messiah? Save yourself and us.' His words carried the language and tone of scepticism, cynicism and bitterness. If you are who you say you are, why don't you get us out of this mess? Implied in the taunt is the accusation that Jesus is no better than they are and, like them, his time has run out.

His companion doesn't agree and takes him to task. 'Do you not fear God, since you are under the same condemnation?' Why all this bravado? Have you no shame? With death staring you in the face why are you having a go at him? Besides, we're getting what we deserve, he's innocent, 'This man has done nothing wrong.'

It could be said, with justification, that both criminals were opportunists. The one uses the opportunity to mock and criticize, the other seizes the opportunity to express faith. The fear of the Lord is the beginning of wisdom. The absence of such fear, even in the face of death, leaves one of our Lord's companions without remorse. The presence of such fear in the other brings him to the point of penitence and faith which results in an amazing request, 'Jesus, remember me when you come into your kingdom.'

Astonishing! A dying man expresses faith in a dying man as someone who will be able to save dying people like himself. Imagine! The one to whom he looks for help is at that moment wearing a crown of thorns. Above his head, written in satirical fashion at the command of Pilate, are the words, 'King of the Jews'. A less kingly figure cannot be imagined. Yet it is to this companion in crucifixion that he looks in faith. And his request of faith is answered with promptness and with a promise far beyond his expectations. 'Truly I tell you,' said Jesus, 'today you will be with me in Paradise.'

The grace of God always exceeds our expectations. The thief only asks to be remembered when Jesus comes in his kingly power. He is told that before the day is out he will be with Jesus in Paradise, the place of the righteous dead. Thus the ministry of Jesus was continuing, despite the constrictions of crucifixion. Three times he has been mocked with, 'Save yourself', with one criminal adding 'and us'. Saving himself was not an option. Saving others was what he had come to do and so a criminal who began the day as a social outcast ends it in the company of the Saviour of the world.

But there remains a mystery. There were two criminals and the Son of God was within speaking distance of both. The grace of God was available and adequate to save both, but only one received the promise. Why? Speculation on such matters is rarely profitable. Perhaps we are left simply to reflect upon the grace of God. One of the features of Luke's Gospel is its emphasis on the saving love of Jesus reaching out to those whom society has rejected. The promise of Jesus given to one criminal means that, in the light of the grace of God, none need despair. But by the same token, perhaps, none must ever presume.

'Truly I tell you,' said Jesus, 'today you will be with me in Paradise.'

A passage to read

Luke 23.39–43.

A thought to ponder upon

He that will enter Paradise must have a good key.
(GEORGE HERBERT, QUOTED IN
WARD AND WILD, 1997)

A prayer to use

> O Lord,
> forgive what I have been,
> sanctify what I am,
> and order what I shall be.

Care

> When Jesus saw his mother and the disci-
> ple whom he loved standing beside her,
> he said to his mother, 'Woman, here is
> your son.' Then he said to the disciple,
> 'Here is your mother.' And from that hour
> the disciple took her into his own home.
>
> (JOHN 19.26–7)

When the death of someone close to us is imminent, several voices clamour for our attention. There are the voices of memory and sorrow, hope and despair and, sometimes, bitterness and anger. The mother of Jesus must have been aware of some of these voices as she stood in the shadow of the cross. But there may have been one voice above all others that claimed her attention and that was the voice of prophecy.

When Mary, with Joseph and the infant Jesus, came to

the Temple for the customary rituals of purification and presentation they were met by a man called Simeon. He was a person of great age and piety. The Spirit of God filled his life and revealed to him that before he died he would see God's promised Messiah. Not only did he see him, he also held him in his arms and praised God with a wonderful song which began, 'Lord now you let your servant go in peace, your word has been fulfilled'.

To say the least, Mary and Joseph were amazed at some of the things he said about Jesus and none was more amazing than his prophecy to Mary, 'This child is destined for the falling and the rising of many in Israel, and to be a sign that will be opposed so that the inner thoughts of many will be revealed – and a sword will pierce your own soul too' (Luke 2.25–35). We are not told what Mary's reaction was to these words. She simply stored them up in her heart.

As the years went by, however, the meaning of Simeon's words began to take shape on a variety of occasions. Mary felt their force, for instance, when the gossipmongers of Nazareth raised questions about Jesus' birth and parentage. She was hurt deeply when people misunderstood Jesus and her other children questioned his sanity. And we can imagine her pain when his first sermon in his home synagogue ended in near tragedy. She must have longed for the day when he would be vindicated, when his true identity would be revealed.

But now, at Calvary, the prophecy of Simeon is being fulfilled as never before. Her son is despised and rejected, forsaken by friends and forgotten, it seems, by God. It was to such sorrow, loneliness and grief that Jesus directed his third word from the cross. At the moment when he is involved with the great cosmic struggle with the powers of darkness Jesus Christ makes time to provide for the immediate and future needs of his mother. Speaking to his mother and to his beloved disciple John, he says, 'Woman, here is your son' and 'Son, here is your mother.' 'From that hour,' we are told, 'that disciple took her into his own home.'

There is a simple yet profound message here. Jesus drew no false distinction between the natural and the spiritual. Being so preoccupied with his own personal suffering he might have been excused if he had overlooked the needs of his mother. Bearing in mind the stupendous nature of what he was accomplishing through the cross perhaps he could be forgiven if he had forgotten the ties of nature. But no! The fact that we may have great responsibility in so-called spiritual work, or any other kind of work for that matter, does not relieve us from our duty to those of our own flesh and blood. It is true for us, as it was for Jesus, that holiness does not flourish on the basis of neglected family responsibilities.

The only other occasion on which Jesus mentioned his mother was at the marriage in Cana (John 2.4). There, when she tried to play a part in his ministry, he rebuked her with the words, 'My hour has not yet come.' But now his 'hour' has come. He has 'finished' his unique task (John 19.30). And, from the cross, he gives a specific task to his mother. Whatever our understanding of that task it must not exclude a proper and biblical recognition of the significance of the place that Mary has occupied in Christian spirituality in the Church and down the centuries.

Mother, here is your son.
Son, here is your mother.

Passages to read

John 2.1–11.
John 19.25–7.

A thought to ponder upon

> She gave her body for God's shrine,
> Her heart to piercing pain,
> And knew the cost of love divine
> When Jesus Christ was slain.
>
> (J. R. PEACHEY, 1896–1971)

A prayer to use

> God,
> give me a practical holiness
> that places family responsibilities
> within the circle of my love for you.

Dereliction

> About three o'clock Jesus cried with a
> loud voice. 'Eli, Eli, lema sabachthani?'
> that is, 'My God, my God, why have you
> forsaken me?'
>
> (MATTHEW 27.46)

Jesus had been on the cross for three hours. Suddenly, at noon, the situation changes dramatically. The hill of Calvary and the city of Jerusalem are embraced with a darkness that can be felt. At this point even the seasoned crucifixion watchers must have realized that this was an execution with a difference. They have not experienced a darkness like this before. It is ironic that the one who came to be the light of the world should spend his final hours in darkness.

Is the darkness a symbol of evil at work? Is it a sign of the judgement of God? Is it nature's way of identifying itself with events that have significance for the whole world? We can suggest, we can conjecture, we can reflect – but we don't know. There is a mysteriousness about the darkness that we do well to respect. When faced with a mystery, silence is usually more important than speech, though silence may have been part of the suffering being endured by Jesus. At other significant moments of his ministry he had heard his Father's voice from heaven offering him reassurance and approval. On this occasion the voice of God remains silent.

But, after three hours of darkness, Jesus can no longer remain silent and he pierces the darkness with this heart-rending cry of dereliction, 'My God, my God, why have you forsaken me?' With this cry from the lips of Jesus, it takes little imagination to believe that we are probably at the climax of his suffering. In all that he had suffered at the hands of opponents not one cry of pain or complaint had crossed his lips. But such is the nature of the transaction that is taking place between himself and God he can keep silent no longer and this cry of anguish is torn from him.

Our response to such words can only be one of reverence and humility. The place whereon we stand is holy ground. We know, of course, that they are the opening words of Psalm 22. But they seem so strange, almost blasphemous, on the lips of Jesus, who had come from God and was going to God. How are we to understand them without appearing either arrogant or insensitive? The one thing we must not do is explain them away. The words come not just from Psalm 22 but from a broken heart. Jesus feels forsaken by God.

Has God, as it were, turned his back on him? Does the fact that he is at this moment bearing the sins of the world mean that he is cut off from God's presence? That may be part of the mystery. Yet Paul, when writing to the Christians at Corinth, said that, 'In Christ God was reconciling the world to himself' (2 Corinthians 5.19). Can God really take leave of absence at this crucial moment? May it not be that God's silence, far from indicating his absence, means that he is present but the darkness is also affecting him, that the crucifixion is also being experienced by him?

These are truly deep waters. But did not God say to his people of old that when they passed through the waters of trial and affliction he would be with them (Isaiah 43.2)? Does the promise not also apply to Jesus at Calvary? God is no distant spectator of the crucifixion; he identifies with it. He is not immune to suffering; he endures it alongside Jesus. He doesn't stand aloof from the darkness; he is right there in the middle of it.

We may never be able to penetrate the depth of the mystery of our Lord's cry of dereliction but it holds for me a personal paradox. I am humbled that he endured such suffering to bring about the salvation of humankind, myself included. Amazing grace! At the same time I am encouraged that Jesus echoed the words that so many lonely, bewildered and desolate people have uttered throughout the ages. Forsakeness is an appalling experience. Jesus knows – from the inside. Amazing love!

My God, my God, why have you forsaken me?

Passages to read

Matthew 27.45–9.
Mark 15.33–6.

A thought to ponder upon

Even the most beautiful community can never heal the wound of loneliness that we carry. It is only when we

discover that this loneliness can become a sacrament
that we touch wisdom, for this sacrament is purification
and presence of God.

(JEAN VANIER, FOUNDER OF THE L'ARCHE COMMUNITY,
QUOTED IN WARD AND WILD, 1997)

A prayer to use

Lord,
hold in your love all who are crushed by loneliness,
    help them to know your presence
    and to believe your promise
that you will never leave them nor forsake them.

Thirst

> After this, when Jesus knew that all was
> now finished, he said (in order to fulfil the
> scripture), 'I am thirsty.'
>
> (JOHN 19.28)

It is not surprising that Jesus is thirsty. From the moment
of his arrest he has been hustled back and forth across
Jerusalem, from Gethsemane to the house of Caiaphas and
from there to Pilate's residence, then on to Herod, and back
again to Pilate. And all the while suffering interrogation by
the religious and civil authorities, together with insults,
beatings, scourging and the farce of a trial.

Finally, he is made to walk the emotional and painful
path to Golgotha where he endures the physical agony of
crucifixion and the mental and spiritual torment symbolized by the three hours of darkness. Small wonder he is
thirsty.

His request for a drink is natural, but none the less

amazing. The maker of heaven and earth has parched lips. His earthly ministry had begun with 40 days of hunger in the wilderness. It ends with raging thirst on a Roman gibbet. What are we to make of it? Clearly, it speaks of his humanity. Like other human beings he hungers and thirsts, suffers pain and hardship and, when necessary, looks to others for help. Yet, we know there is more to it than that. The words, 'I am thirsty' are not forced out of him. They come by his own volition.

John tells us (18.1ff.) that on the night before he died Jesus took his disciples across the Kidron Valley, which divides the city from the Mount of Olives, to a garden which they probably used for peace and quiet while staying in Jerusalem. Judas knew where to find him, therefore, when he led the authorities to Jesus after his betrayal. Having 'gone out into the night' during the Last Supper, he now turns up with the agents of darkness, the Roman soldiers and Jewish police, who combine to take Jesus prisoner. Peter tries to prevent them with an over-hasty use of a sword. He is told by Jesus to put it away and given an explanation why: 'Am I not to drink the cup the Father has given me?' Those words, I believe, suggest an important part of the meaning behind the words, 'I am thirsty.'

The cup which the Father has placed in his hands is a bitter one. It involves the giving of his life for the life of the world. It involves allowing evil and darkness to do its worst and showing how it may be overcome, through self-giving love. He does not shrink from the drinking of that cup. On the contrary, he is eager to drink it to the very dregs. So, when he has made provision for his beloved mother and his beloved disciple and through them, perhaps, for the new post-resurrection community, he perceives that he has finished all he had come to do and says, 'I am thirsty.'

It is an expression of his desire to obey his Father's will

to which he had committed himself at the beginning of his ministry and again, so dramatically, in Gethsemane: 'Not what I want, but what you want.' So he says, 'I am thirsty.' I am thirsty and will remain thirsty until the job is done, the cup is empty, the will of my Father is accomplished. Only when he has tasted the bitter wine of death can his Father's will be fulfilled.

And there is yet another layer of meaning for us to reflect upon. The only other time he asked for a drink in John's Gospel was from the Samaritan woman at the well of Sychar (John 4.7ff.). On that occasion Jesus had referred to himself as the giver of 'living water'. Here he is once more expressing his thirst – his thirst to complete God's will and work so that the 'living water', his own risen life conveyed through his Spirit, will become available for all humankind. He is thirsty to complete the task which will release that living water that will eternally satisfy those who drink it. As he said to the woman at the well of Sychar, 'Those who drink of the water that I shall give them will never be thirsty. The water that I shall give will become in them a spring of water gushing up to eternal life.'

I am thirsty.

Passages to read

John 19.28–30.
John 4.7–15.

A thought to ponder upon

Feed upon the will of God and drink the chalice of Jesus with your eyes shut, so that you may not see what is inside.

(PAUL OF THE CROSS, 1694–1775, QUOTED IN
WARD AND WILD, 1997)

A prayer to use

I heard the voice of Jesus say,
'Behold, I freely give
the living water; thirsty one,
stoop down and drink, and live':
I came to Jesus, and I drank
of that life-giving stream;
my thirst was quenched, my soul revived,
and now I live in Him.

(J. B. DYKES, 1823, ANGLICAN HYMN BOOK)

Finished

When Jesus had received the wine, he said, 'It is finished.' Then he bowed his head and gave up his spirit.

(JOHN 19.30)

My two-year-old grandson has a star turn which invariably pleases his grandparents, especially when they are babysitting. He knows that it brings a smile to their faces and a 'good boy' to their lips, so he is always ready to perform. He takes his cup, drinks whatever juice or milk that is in it and then, with a smack of his lips, holds it upside down and says, 'All gone.' He hasn't yet learned to say, 'It is finished', but his actions leave us in no doubt. The inverted cup speaks volumes. 'All gone.' Finished! There is not one drop left. That simple yet immensely profound truth is at the heart of our Lord's penultimate word from the cross, 'It is finished.'

He had been crucified at 9 a.m. At noon, the city of Jerusalem and the hill of Calvary were enveloped in a deep darkness for the space of three hours. So it is after nearly six hours on the cross that Jesus cries, 'It is finished.' Some of the bystanders might have interpreted it as a cry of despair and failure. Nothing could be further from the truth. In the original Greek it is just one word *tetelestai* – not a word of defeat but of victory. The word that an athlete might use as he crossed the finishing line. 'I've made it. I've finished the course.' It is in this word, perhaps more than any other, that the essence of the Gospel is contained.

On the lips of Jesus the word certainly means that his suffering is at an end. Death was coming in a matter of moments. But to limit the meaning of the word as referring only to the end of his six-hour physical ordeal, would be unwise. It has to do with a far greater time-span than that. His suffering is the culmination of a lifetime of perfect obedience to his Father's will.

The cross didn't take him by surprise. He had been born, as it were, in the shadow of the cross. He had lived his life and exercised his ministry in anticipation of it. He had warned his followers again and again that it must be so, 'The Son of Man must undergo great suffering' (Mark 8.31). He knew that the accumulated guilt of humanity would meet on him, for only then could he fulfil the meaning of his name and the purpose of his birth, 'You are to call him Jesus, for he will save his people from their sins' (Matthew 1.21). Knowing all these things he still refused to turn away from the cross. Self-giving and sacrifice was his chosen way.

So when Jesus says, 'It is finished', he means that his journey is over. He has walked the pathway of obedience to the very end of the road. But more than that, he has offered the sacrifice to end all sacrifice. For centuries the people of God had looked for acceptance with God through an elaborate system of sacrifice. But such sacrifices were meant to be temporary and transient. They pointed to and prepared the way for a sacrifice that was both perfect and permanent.

It was that sacrifice, the sacrifice of himself for the sins of all, that Jesus offered on the cross. And having offered it he said, 'It is finished.' The old sacrificial system is ended. The perfect sacrifice had been offered, there is no need for any other.

Jesus has finished the work which his Father had given him to do (see also John 17.4). He has accomplished all that his Father had desired. Every aspect of the will of his Father has been obeyed. Every obstacle between humankind and God has been removed. Because of what Jesus has accomplished on the cross all can find acceptance with God.

Like an artist when he puts the finishing touch to the picture on the canvas and lays aside his brush, there can be no further improvement, there is nothing more to be added. So Jesus says, 'It is finished' and lays down his life.

Passages to read

John 19.28–30.
Hebrews 10.11–23.

A thought to ponder upon

There must be a beginning of any great matter, but the continuing unto the end until it be thoroughly finished yields the true glory.

(FRANCIS DRAKE, QUOTED IN WARD AND WILD, 1997)

A prayer to use

Here let me prove your perfect will,
my acts of faith and love repeat,
till death your endless mercies seal
and make the sacrifice complete!

(CHARLES WESLEY, 1707–88)

Commendation

> Then Jesus, crying with a loud voice, said,
> 'Father, into your hands I commend my
> spirit.' Having said this, he breathed his
> last.
>
> (LUKE 23.46)

The serenity that marked the life of Jesus did not forsake
him at the point of death. There is no anger, no distress, no
loss of dignity. Instead there is a calmness and a control
that speaks volumes for his trust in God his Father. The
mysterious cry of dereliction and apparent separation is
replaced by a sense of assured communion with the Father.
The Son of God moves with purpose and confidence
towards death and on his lips are words from Psalm 31 (v.5)
as he commits his spirit into the hands of his Father.

His death, when it came, took the soldiers by surprise.
They had had a long day and wanted to complete their duty
before nightfall, so they followed the customary procedure
for hurrying death along by breaking the legs of the crucified. In the case of Jesus they were too late.

He had said earlier in his ministry that no one could take
his life from him, 'I have power to lay it down and I have
power to take it up again' (John 10.18). The truth of those
words is beautifully and movingly illustrated in the final
moments of his earthly life. He is not the passive victim of
other people's manipulative power. The civil and ecclesias-
tical authorities, personified in people like Pilate and
Caiaphas, imagine that they are in control. But no! There is
something much greater, and universally more significant,
taking place than their petty prejudices will allow them to
see.

The action of Jesus in giving his life is an act of complete
freedom and filial obedience. The Father gave the Son for

the life of the world, now the Son gives back his life to the Father. The glory or character of God is revealed in total self-giving between the Father and the Son. What a contrast to the self-protective attitudes of those who had combined to put an end to his life of selfless love.

The words, 'Father, into your hands I commend my spirit', are not whispered in weakness. They were spoken loudly, with conviction and head held erect. Only when they are spoken does he bow his head and take his final breath. But Luke, in his record of events, doesn't leave it there. He takes us behind the scenes, as it were, and reveals some interesting responses to our Lord's death.

The Roman centurion in charge of the crucifixion is deeply affected by all that he has seen and heard. He praises God and says, 'Certainly this man was innocent.' Watching the deadly conflict between Jesus and the Jewish authorities who have handed him over to Roman justice, he becomes convinced that it is Jesus rather than the religious leaders who are in touch with God. The obvious presence of God with this man from Galilee has a profound influence on him.

Something deep and discerning has also been taking place within the crowd who came to see the crucifixion as a spectacle. Perhaps they were not able to assess fully what has happened to them during their time at Calvary. But whatever it is, they go home in a different frame of mind to the one in which they came. 'They returned home, beating their breasts.' Such action is a sign of mourning. They know it has been a sad day for Israel, and for them – for they are not blameless (see also John 19.13–23).

Others, however, remain where they have stood all day, a small group of faithful followers of Jesus, including women. Understandably, they are dejected. They had invested so much hope in him and the vision he had shared with them. That hope is now dead and the future is unsure.

They have stayed at the cross out of love and loyalty and, remarkably, they make a vital contribution to a future filled with hope. Their eye-witness account of the incontrovertible fact that he has died served only to lend credibility to the testimony of those among them who became the first witnesses to his resurrection.

Finally, something else was happening that went to the very core of the religious structures. 'The curtain of the temple was torn in two.' The curtain which hid the symbolic presence of God into which only the High Priest could enter, and then only once a year, is torn in two. The way into the presence of God is now open to all.

Such is the achievement of the life and death of Jesus. Such also is the source of our confidence in life and in death, to be held in the hands of God – the safest place in all the world to be!

Father, into your hands I commend my spirit.

Passages to read

Luke 23.44–55.
Hebrews 9.5–12.

A thought to ponder upon

Death is the supreme festival on the road to freedom.

(DIETRICH BONHOEFFER, QUOTED IN
WARD AND WILD, 1997)

A prayer to use

O Lord, you have made us very small, and we bring our years to an end like a tale that is told; help us to remember that beyond our brief day is the eternity of your love.

(REINHOLD NIEBUHR, 1892–1972)

6

Christ is risen

Jesus Christ is risen today,
Alleluia,
our triumphant holy day;
alleluia,
who did once upon the cross
alleluia,
suffer to redeem our loss.
alleluia!

(HYMNS FOR TODAY'S CHURCH)

He is not here

Do not be afraid; I know that you are looking for Jesus who was crucified. He is not here; for he has been raised, as he said. Come and see the place where he lay.

(MATTHEW 28.5–6)

Songs of triumph and joy invariably mark Easter morning services in Christian churches throughout the world. Even at the increasingly popular 'sunrise services', when many worshippers are barely awake, there is an unmistakable note of happiness and victory as they praise the risen Lord.

But it wasn't like that on the first Easter morning. Alarm, fear and bewilderment were the emotions that rose to the surface as the followers of Jesus, having come early to the tomb, were told, 'He is not here.'

At first they couldn't believe it. The two Marys had come to administer the funeral rites to a corpse. They had brought spices to anoint the body of Jesus. They had watched him die. They had watched him laid in the tomb. There hadn't been time before nightfall on Good Friday to perform these acts of devotion. So they arose very early on the morning after the Jewish sabbath and, while it was still dark, hurried to the tomb – and got two almighty shocks.

The first concerned the stone. Ever since they saw the body of Jesus laid in the tomb provided by Joseph of Arimathea they had been obsessed by the stone. How on earth were they going to shift it? It had probably taken several soldiers to roll it into place so we can understand their anxiety as they approached the tomb, 'Who will roll away the stone for us from the entrance of the tomb? (Mark 16.3). They needn't have worried. Matthew tells us that by the time they got there the stone had been rolled away and an angel of the Lord was sitting on it!

On Friday night it seemed that the stone, to change the metaphor, was the final nail in the coffin. A symbol of a society that had dispatched for ever this would-be Messiah, this upstart peasant carpenter from Nazareth. 'We've put paid to this pretentious preacher.' Now that stone was being 'sat upon'! An amusing indication, perhaps, of what God thought of their attempt to keep his Son, the Prince of Life, dead and buried in a tomb.

But the shock of the stone being rolled away literally opened up the way for an even greater shock. Having worried about the presence of the stone, they now began to worry about its absence! Immediately, however, they are reassured by the messenger of God, 'Don't be afraid, I know you are looking for Jesus who was crucified, he is not here; for he has been raised, as he said. Come and see the place were he lay.'

Suddenly it was not just the stone that was turned upside down, their categories of thought were turned upside down. They didn't need the spices they had brought. There was no body to anoint. They wouldn't be returning home to mourn their dead friend. Instead they were being sent with the message that he was alive. 'Go quickly and tell his disciples, "He has been raised from the dead, and indeed he is going ahead of you into Galilee: there you will see him," this is my message for you.'

What a turn around! One minute, gloom, doom and sad intent, the next, surprise, wonder and joyful purpose. They had hurried to the tomb with spices, now they ran with the message that the tomb was empty. But the morning of shocks wasn't over yet As they went to deliver the good news, the good news suddenly stood in front of them. The one whose dead body they had gone to anoint now stands before them alive and well. He greeted them and they grabbed hold of his feet – a customary act of devout worship.

But it must also have been a moment of overwhelming joy. They had seen the empty tomb, but of itself the empty tomb is insufficient evidence of the resurrection. Now they see and hold the risen Lord himself. The message they are carrying has become reality. It is true what the angels have said. It is true what he promised on the way to the cross. Jesus has been raised from the dead. His presence before them is a vindication of all he had said and done during his ministry. Their hope in Jesus has not been misplaced. He is indeed the Son of God. Even death cannot hold him. Their whole life, past, present and future, is radically changed. The past is forgiven, the future is secure, the present is alive with the life of God.

Christ is risen. He is risen indeed. Alleluia!

Passages to read

Matthew 28.1–10.
Mark 16.1–8.

A thought to ponder upon

Women were the first witnesses to and messengers of the resurrection of Jesus Christ from the dead.

A prayer to use

Thine be the glory, risen conquering Son,
endless is the victory Thou o'er death hast won;
angels in bright raiment rolled the stone away,
kept the folded grave-clothes where Thy body lay.

Thine be the glory, risen conquering Son,
    endless is the victory Thou o'er death hast won.

(ANGLICAN HYMN BOOK)

Behind closed doors

> When it was evening on that day, the first
> day of the week, and the doors of the
> house where the disciples had met were
> locked for fear of the Jews, Jesus came and
> stood among them and said, 'Peace be
> with you.'

(JOHN 20.19)

Two were missing. One of them, Judas, was dead by his own
hand. The other, Thomas, just hadn't turned up. He was
having a crisis of faith. But the other disciples were present
once again in that upper room in Jerusalem. We know
nothing of their conversation. The words of Jesus, 'Peace be
with you', was the ordinary Jewish greeting. But this was no
ordinary day. The words assumed special significance and
spoke with pertinence and power to their state of mind.

It is not difficult to imagine some of the things that had
risen to the surface of their thoughts. Their failure of nerve,
for instance, during the events leading to the crucifixion
would still rankle. The report from some, of the empty tomb
and the appearance of Jesus, would be a source of burgeon-
ing hope mingled with anxiety lest it should prove false.
And there was the underlying fear of what the Jews might
still do in their efforts to destroy the memory of Jesus. They
were in need of peace and reassurance.

It was to this condition of heart and mind that Jesus

spoke his word of peace and backed it up with a graphic visual aid, 'He showed them his hands and his side.' By these marks they are able to identify the one who stood before them as Jesus. It is the same Jesus whom they forsook – yet he speaks not criticism but peace to them. It is the same Jesus who was crucified and is now with them again – the story of the resurrection is true. It is the same Jesus who was laid in the tomb, for these are the marks of death and he has conquered it – there is nothing to fear.

These are not just nice thoughts. They are immensely important truths for the *shalom* or true well-being of all humankind. The Christian faith declares that 'The Crucified is *the risen Lord* and the risen Lord *is the Crucified.*' Nothing can alter that. Jesus has been called a 'flesh and blood' Saviour. His was a real death. His was a real resurrection. His first recorded words to his disciples after his death and resurrection are 'Peace be with you.' It is because Jesus bears the wounds of his decisive battle with evil that he has that peace as his gift and can offer it to his disciples and to whoever will receive it. The fact that he links his words with his wounds is an indication that his death and resurrection are the means of saving the whole person and the whole world.

Small wonder that 'The disciples rejoiced when they saw the Lord.' His presence not only brought reassurance, it also fulfilled a promise. As the disciples grew ever more fearful in the shadow of his impending crucifixion he had promised that he would see them again and their pain would turn into joy (John 16.16–24). He kept his word and brought joy to their hearts.

But the wounds of the crucified risen Lord are not only linked with the peace he offered his disciples but also with the commission he gave them. 'Peace be with you,' he said to them again, and added these amazing words, 'As the

Father has sent me, so I send you.' They are to continue his work and mission in the world. His gift of peace is not for them alone. They were to take it into the life of the world around them.

That is a daunting task, after all it cost him his life. They will need, therefore, the special help of his Holy Spirit. So he gives them another visual aid to reassure them. 'He breathed on them and said, "Receive the Holy Spirit. If you forgive the sins of any, they are forgiven them; if you retain the sins of any, they are retained."'

Volumes have been written to explain the meaning of these words, which indicates that there is room for confusion and contradiction. But of two things I am certain. First, the linking of these words with the wounds of the risen Jesus is significant. It accords with the truth proclaimed elsewhere in John's Gospel that when Jesus was glorified the Spirit would be given (7.39). Jesus, having completed the work his Father gave him to do, is now glorified and therefore gives his Spirit to those who will continue his mission in the world.

Second, his mission has to do with the forgiveness of sins. At the beginning of his ministry he was described as 'The Lamb of God who takes away the sin of the world' (John 1.29). God has in Jesus Christ taken away the sin of the world. Now he commissions the Church, in the power of his Spirit, to give effect to that truth in its life and witness. To declare and pronounce forgiveness where it is appropriate and to shine the light of judgement on those areas of society were guilt is unacknowledged and unconfessed. Such a ministry requires the help of the Spirit.

A passage to read

John 20.19–23.

A thought to ponder upon

Through Jesus, 'God was pleased to reconcile to himself all things, whether on earth or in heaven, by making peace through the blood of his cross.'

(COLOSSIANS 1.20)

A prayer to use

O God,
by the power of your Spirit, help me
to speak peace to those in turmoil
and bring peace to those in trouble.

Risen but not recognized

While they were walking and discussing, Jesus himself came near and went with them, but their eyes were kept from recognizing him.

(LUKE 24.15–16)

The same only different. It sounds contradictory but it is true. The Jesus who died and rose again was the same – but different. He was not immediately recognizable. Mary mistook him for the gardener until he called her name (John 20.11–18). The disciples needed the sight of his wounds to assure them of his identity. Cleopas and his companion walked and talked with him for miles on the evening of the resurrection before they recognized their fellow traveller as their risen Lord.

Their seven-mile journey from Jerusalem to Emmaus embraces one of the finest stories in the whole of literature.

Like all the records of the resurrection appearances it is full of mystery yet, at the same time, it touches the human spirit in the most practical ways. We don't quite know, for instance, the manner in which 'their eyes were kept from recognizing him'. But we do know, from this encounter on the Emmaus road, that God comes to people where they are and as they are. To the travellers on the road he comes as a fellow traveller and walks alongside them.

As Jesus meets up with them and joins in their conversation we have the irony of his being gently chided as the only person ignorant of the things that had taken place in Jerusalem during the past three days! His question, 'What things?' opens up the way for them to tell their story, which is really the gospel story. They recount the good news of God's generosity in sending Jesus to bring life to the world and how it was met by humankind's refusal to welcome him. Instead he was crucified.

At this point Cleopas and his companion insert a very revealing sentence into their story, 'We had hoped that he was the one to redeem Israel.' Then, having shared some further news about a possible resurrection from those who had seen the empty tomb, they inserted another revealing sentence, 'but him they did not see'. Those two sentences revealed their state of mind. They were disillusioned. They were returning home with their hopes dashed and their dreams shattered. Though they were talking about Jesus, to Jesus, they have somehow allowed their own agenda to rise to the surface. Their crushed hopes and, perhaps a little self-pity, have taken centre stage.

Jesus gently but firmly removes them from that stage, 'Oh, how foolish you are, and how slow of heart to believe all that the prophets have declared. Was it not necessary that the Messiah should suffer these things and then enter into his glory?' Then, with superb insight, sensitivity and skill, he revealed how the Old Testament, at its heart, is a story about Jesus. He put the events of recent days in Jerusalem, to which they had referred with such despondency, into the perspective of God. Far from indicating that hope was gone, they were to become the source of all hope. The cross does not mean that all is lost. On the contrary, in the light of the resurrection, it means that all is under control – the sovereign control of God.

When Cleopas and his companion later recalled that conversation with Jesus on the journey they spoke in terms of the Scriptures being opened and their hearts being set on fire. It is interesting, therefore, to note that their first action after such an extraordinary experience was to offer hospitality to this stranger whom they still failed to recognize as the risen Jesus. So Jesus enters their home to stay the night and the climax of this wonderful story is reached.

As they shared a meal with Jesus three things happened, 'their eyes were opened, and they recognized him; and he vanished out of their sight'. Again, we are confronting mystery. The blockage to recognition, whatever it was, is removed. The stranger is Jesus who, although he is the guest, acts as the host and performs the same four actions as he did at the Last Supper. He takes the bread, blesses it, breaks it, and gives it to them.

Was that meal a Eucharist? It was certainly a sacrament, for they later testified to the disciples that Jesus 'had been made known to them in the breaking of the bread'. Like Christians today they experienced Christ in word and sacrament. He came to them through the Scriptures on the road. He came to them at table in their home. But, immediately they recognized him, he vanished from their sight. He was indeed the same only different. His former earthly limitations had gone. So too had their natural tiredness. They rushed back to Jerusalem with the good news only to discover that the good news had outrun them. Peter also had met with the risen Lord. Jesus was alive and on the move!

A passage to read

Luke 24.13–35.

A thought to ponder upon

He meets with us in every circumstance and walks beside us on the road of life.

(GEORGE ELIOT)

A prayer to use

Risen Christ,
help me to see your presence
not only in word and sacrament
but also in the lives and needs of other people.

Second time round

A week later his disciples were again in
the house, and Thomas was with them.
Although the doors were shut, Jesus came
and stood among them and said, 'Peace be
with you.'

(JOHN 20.26)

The grace of God is flexible. It makes allowances for our moods and, it seems, even for our diaries! Thomas was missing on that first occasion after the resurrection when Jesus appeared to his disciples in Jerusalem. So he missed out on the blessing Jesus gave them, but not for long. One week later Jesus returned for the sake of Thomas. It was an experience worth waiting for. Indeed, humankind would be the poorer if the dramatic encounter between Thomas and the risen Jesus had never taken place.

All too often Thomas gets a bad press. As a character he is much maligned and tends to be remembered, and enshrined in folk lore, as 'doubting Thomas'. But there is much more to him than that. He was a person of courage and integrity, willing to die with Jesus (John 11.16) and prepared to question Jesus rather than pretend he knew all the answers (John 14.5). But, undoubtedly, he was a determined member of the 'awkward squad'. This was clearly demonstrated in his confrontation with the other disciples after the first appearance of Jesus to them.

They, seeing the wounds of Jesus, had recognized their Lord and believed. When they told Thomas, however, his reaction was far from compliant. He not only reserved judgement, he also laid down somewhat violent and rather outrageous conditions if he was to believe. Thomas, it seemed, wanted to be in control of the situation and to determine the criteria for faith. 'Unless I see the mark of the nails in his hands, and put my finger in the mark of the nails and my hand in his side, I will not believe.' Unlike the other disciples, seeing will not suffice. He must both see and touch.

But the grace of God is flexible. Not only does Jesus return to that room in Jerusalem with the greeting, 'Peace be with you', but he also invites Thomas to do as he had insisted he must do. 'Put your finger here and see my hands. Reach out your hand and put it in my side. Do not doubt but believe.'

Perhaps, the grace of the invitation coupled with the charge of unbelief was enough. Perhaps, Thomas suddenly realized the insensitivity of his insistence that he touch those places which unbelievers had so forcefully touched in crucifixion. We may never know. But, whatever the cause, the barriers of doubt and unbelief came down. So much so, that there is no record of Thomas touching Jesus in the way he had earlier insisted he must. Instead, in answer to the invitation and challenge thrown down by Jesus, there came this magnificent confession of faith, 'My Lord and my God!'

There is an interesting insight here regarding the significance of Thomas's contribution as a disciple of Jesus. I once heard an Irish friend of mine being described as a 'profitable inconvenience'. I thought, at first, it was a term of ridicule. I discovered through experience, however, that it was a term of admiration. My Irish friend was a person who made a difference.

Thomas was that kind of person. His somewhat aggressive response to the words of Jesus, 'You know the way to the place where I am going,' was typical. 'Lord, we do not know where you are going. How can we know the way?' As a result of this forthright honesty we now possess one of the classic sayings of Jesus, 'I am the way, and the truth, and the life' (John 14.6). Likewise, his determination to set his own criteria for faith was somewhat questionable, but it resulted in a classic confession of faith and, indeed, summed up the message of the Gospel of John. The man from Nazareth is 'My Lord and my God.'

Thomas, through his honesty and courage to doubt and to question, has stretched through the ages and touched your life and mine in a unique way. Unlike him we have not seen the Lord in the flesh nor, indeed, gazed at the marks of the passion in his hands and side. Nevertheless, because of Thomas, Jesus Christ has reserved a blessing for us. 'Have you believed because you have seen me?' said Jesus to Thomas after his great confession. 'Blessed are those who have not seen and yet have come to believe.' The risen Lord returned for Thomas and in doing so gave encouragement and hope to all who, with integrity and courage, struggle towards resurrection faith.

A passage to read

John 20.24–9.

A thought to ponder upon

Faith is the capacity to live with doubt.

A prayer to use

> Christ our Saviour, Son of the Father,
>   crucified and alive for ever;
> grant us the faith which doubts not your word,
> trusts where it cannot see,
> and rests in your love and mercy
> now and for ever. Amen.

Breakfast by the sea

> When they had finished breakfast, Jesus
> said to Simon Peter, 'Simon son of John,
> do you love me more than these?' He said
> to him, 'Yes, Lord; you know that I love
> you.' Jesus said to him, 'Feed my lambs.'
>
> (JOHN 21.15)

There was unfinished business between Peter and Jesus. They had sparked off each other on occasion (see also Matthew 21.22–3) but Jesus still held to his prediction and promise that Peter would become a pillar of his Church. However, it looked as if Peter's abject, threefold denial of Jesus on the night before he died, had put an end to all that. The look from Jesus as the cock crowed had driven him to tears. It seemed that the Lord's confident estimate of his potential was in urgent need of revision.

Then had come that sensitive and compassionate instruction to the two Marys from the messenger of God (Mark 16.7). Having seen the empty tomb and heard the news that Jesus had been raised from the dead, they were sent to tell the disciples and Peter. In that message there lies the promise of forgiveness and a fresh start for those who had been demoralized and subdued by failure. Before the end of the day those very disciples would be given a renewed call to mission (John 20.19–23).

But there's a hint of a particular poignancy in the words 'and Peter', for he had boasted that though others would forsake and deny Jesus, he never would. Peter was in special need of forgiveness, renewal and reinstatement and Jesus came looking for him for that very purpose. He knew where to find him and there, by the sea of Tiberias, he laid on breakfast for him and the other disciples. But this was to be Peter's special time and, sure enough, after breakfast Jesus gave him his full attention.

It had been beside a charcoal fire that Peter had denied Jesus three times. Now, beside another charcoal fire, he is three times asked the same searching question, 'Do you love me?' It is all part of the unfinished business between them. It was on the Mount of Olives after supper that Peter had claimed that his loyalty to Jesus was greater than those of his fellow disciples. Here, after breakfast by the sea, he is asked if he is prepared to make such a claim now. 'Do you love me more than these?' Peter gets the message. He refuses to compare himself with others. He throws himself on his Lord's knowledge of him for, despite his failure, his love for Jesus remains steadfast: 'Yes, Lord, you know I love you.'

Twice more the question is asked, 'Do you love me?' and twice more Peter answers with an affirmation of his love. But the narrative tells us specifically that 'Peter felt hurt because he said to him the third time, "Do you love me?"'. Was Jesus simply rubbing salt into the wound? Was he making him pay for his base denials? Jesus was not that kind of person. He doesn't extract a promise from Peter of a better performance next time. He was committed to Peter's renewal. He asked the question three times not just to remind him of his denials but in order that three times he might give to this hurt and humbled disciple the commission to care for the flock of God, 'Feed my lambs. Feed my sheep. Feed my sheep.'

Peter's final answer reveals that he has learned his lesson well. He does love his Lord and he is prepared to say so, but he places his confidence not in himself or on the strength of his own love, but on the certainty of Jesus' knowledge. 'Lord, you know everything; you know that I love you.' It was enough. Jesus was so sure of Peter's love that, having told him of the kind of death he would die in glorifying God, said, with complete confidence, 'Follow me.' Jesus was sure of his man!

He also knew that he had recommissioned a sinner, not a saint, and within minutes was sharply rebuking Peter for, literally and metaphorically, looking over his shoulder. Peter, looking behind him, had spotted the Beloved Disciple and said to Jesus, 'Lord, what about him?' Is he going the same way as me? You've told me of my destiny, what about his? Peter is told to mind his own business. He is not to speculate about the discipleship of others. He has only one responsibility, to follow Jesus.

In the forgiveness, renewal and recommissioning of Peter we are given a wonderful illustration of the power of the resurrection and the compassion of the risen Lord. To one who denied him three times with oaths and curses, Jesus gave the responsibility of guiding, guarding and nourishing the flock of God. Failure does not have the last word. There is grace beyond sin. There is hope beyond despair. Thanks be to God!

A passage to read

John 21.15–23.

A thought to ponder upon

Love seeks only one thing; the good of the one loved. It leaves all the other secondary effects to take care of themselves. Love, therefore, is its own reward.

(THOMAS MERTON, QUOTED IN WARD AND WILD, 1997)

A prayer to use

Lord,
help me to love you more
and, in the power of your risen life,
give me grace to express that love
in care and compassion for others.

7

His Spirit is with us

Jesus said, 'I tell you the truth: it
is to your advantage that I go away,
for if I do not go away, the Advocate
will not come to you; but if I go,
I will send him to you.'

(JOHN 16.7)

The unfinished task

> Then the eleven disciples went to
> Galilee, to the mountain where Jesus had
> told them to go. Then Jesus came to them
> and said, 'All authority in heaven and on
> earth has been given to me. Therefore go
> and make disciples of all nations . . .'
>
> (MATTHEW 28.16, 18–19)

When is an ending not the end? is a question that has been
asked in relation to many things over the years. It is the
kind of trick question often found in Christmas crackers
which children take great delight in putting to their parents
and watching them squirm with embarrassment when they
can't produce the answer. I have suffered such humiliation
on many occasions when my children were young, and now
I am having to go through it all again with my grandchildren.
It is fun to play along with the game.

There is a variety of answers, of course, but none is more
accurate than the one supplied on the first Easter morning.
When is an ending not the end? When a dead man bursts
from the tomb!

When the soldiers rolled the stone across the entrance
to the tomb late on Friday afternoon, as far as they were
concerned it marked the end of their day's work – and of
Jesus of Nazareth. The same was true of the disciples. The
thud of the stone as it fell into place marked the end of a
beautiful friendship, the destruction of all their hopes and,
perhaps, a clear indication that they ought to return home,
put the past behind them and get on with the rest of their
lives.

They couldn't have been more mistaken. It was just the
beginning. In the days that followed, the activity of the

risen Jesus literally left them awestruck. He kept turning up in unexpected places to encounter people who were shocked to see him. For each of them, it marked a new beginning.

There was a specific purpose in his post-resurrection appearances. Though unexpected, they were neither random nor haphazard. They were a necessary preparation for what was to come. To be a witness to the resurrection of Jesus Christ was immensely important to the task that lay before his disciples. That is why those who were first at the tomb on that Easter morning were told, 'He is going ahead of you into Galilee, there you will see him just as he told you.'

Galilee was the home of many of them. It was also to be the place of his final farewell to them. But first it was to be the place of commissioning for the work he required them to do in the name of God. They were to continue the work he had begun. It was a tall order for a group of fairly nondescript individuals who were still doubtful, confused and powerless.

So he began by putting his commission to them into divine perspective. 'All authority in heaven and on earth has been given to me.' In other words, the commission I am about to give you is completely in line with the will of God and his eternal purposes for creation, and humankind within it. The word 'therefore' is the key. The commission which they are to receive is in direct consequence of the authority he has been given: 'Therefore go and make disciples of all nations, baptizing them in the name of the Father and of the Son and of the Holy Spirit, and teaching them to obey everything I have commanded you. And surely I am with you always, to the very end of the age.'

In the light of our Lord's claim to sovereign authority, I believe the commission given to the disciples was to influence the world to follow in the way of Christ. It was a commission to win the world for God, not in any militaristic or triumphalist sense, but through the love of Christ so recently demonstrated at Calvary. Did not our Lord say, 'And I, when I am lifted up from the earth, will draw all people to myself'?

It was an awesome responsibility given to the 11 disciples and through them to the whole Church of God. And, as Bishop John V. Taylor has recently claimed, it is a mandate that remains uncancelled. Of course we have to apply the terms of the mandate in a manner which is faithful to the past as well as sensitive and relevant to the present. Nevertheless, it is the unfinished task that the Church is required to pursue to the end of time. Through his death and resurrection Jesus has created a new way for the world. The continuation and completion of the world's history and its ultimate destiny are tied up with Jesus. His way is the way of love. His Church is commissioned to declare and demonstrate that love through its life in every place and in every age. It not only has his authority to do so, it also has the promise of his permanent presence alongside. 'Remember, I am with you always, to the end of the age.'

A passage to read

Matthew 28.16–20.

A thought to ponder upon

Christ cannot live his life today in this world without our mouth, without our eyes, without our going and coming, without our heart. When we love, it is Christ loving through us.

(CARDINAL JOSEPH SUENENS, QUOTED IN
WARD AND WILD, 1997)

A prayer to use

> Lord,
> help me so to walk in your way
> that others may be encouraged to follow.

The final farewell

Then he led them out as far as Bethany,
and, lifting up his hands, he blessed them.
While he was blessing them, he withdrew
from them and was carried up into heaven.

(LUKE 24.50–1)

More than one famous person has said, 'When the curtain falls it is time to leave the stage.' As far as the civil and religious authorities in Jerusalem were concerned, Jesus had left the stage on Good Friday. His disciples believed likewise but subsequent events proved them wrong. Nevertheless, it would have been unhelpful and confusing for the 'flesh and blood' appearances of the risen Jesus to grow fewer and fewer until they simply petered out. There was need for a final farewell.

Jesus had promised there would be one. He had warned them that he would be leaving them but they preferred not to dwell on such a daunting prospect. Indeed, when he said that it was for their sake he was going, they couldn't understand him and were thrown into a panic. 'We don't know what he is talking about,' they said at one point. But that was before the cross. After the resurrection it was different. His appearances changed the atmosphere entirely. So much so that when he did leave them, 'They returned to Jerusalem with great joy; and were continually in the temple blessing God.' The ascension of Jesus, though its full significance may not have been realized until much later, was a source of inspiration and encouragement to them.

The event, as recorded, contains mysterious elements and it is probably unwise to visualize them too literally. We must be careful not to confuse metaphor with fact. The symbolic character and theological meaning of the ascension are more important than any theories of levitation. 'While he was blessing them, he withdrew from them, and was carried up into heaven.' Now, Luke was a gifted writer but he had to use human language. And human speech can never encompass a dimension of reality which is above and beyond our own experience. That's why the accounts of the resurrection appearances vary from one Gospel to another. They were trying to put into words what was beyond words and to describe what was beyond description.

The disciples were sure about one thing, however, and both the resurrection and the ascension confirmed it. Jesus was not only the man from Nazareth, he was also the Son of God from heaven. From heaven he had come and to heaven he now returned – scars and all. Just as he came from heaven and took our humanity so he went back to heaven and took our humanity with him. Their friend on earth had become their friend in heaven. In the light of these things it is not surprising that they went back to Jerusalem full of joy and praise to God.

But, as the rest of the New Testament makes clear, there was much more to it than that. The Jesus of earth had become the Christ of heaven. Here is how St Paul described the resurrection and ascension, both of which he saw as God the Father's response to the obedience of his Son in his self-giving on the cross:

> Therefore God also highly exalted him
> and gave him the name
> that is above every name,

> so that at the name of Jesus
>> every knee should bend,
>> in heaven and on earth and under
>>> the earth,
>> and every tongue should confess
>> that Jesus Christ is Lord,
>> to the glory of God the Father.

The One who was lifted up on the cross to die, and lifted up from the tomb to live, had now been lifted up into heaven to reign. By raising him from death and exalting him to glory God had shown his approval of the life that Jesus had lived. There must have been times during their discipleship with Jesus when those who followed him so devotedly had second thoughts. In the long shadow of the cross there were signs of uncertainty that the Jesus way was the true way (Matthew 16.22). The resurrection and ascension were God's hallmark on the life of Jesus. They affirmed God's right way of living. They are a vindication of a particular way of living in obedience to God and in love with other human beings. As the disciples journeyed back to Jerusalem they must have felt encouraged to continue to follow in the Jesus way.

Luke began his Gospel account in Jerusalem, with a scene in the temple at the hour of worship. It created an atmosphere of anticipation. Something unique was about to happen. And it did – Jesus came. At the close of the Gospel we are again in Jerusalem, in the temple, at the hour of worship. The disciples are worshipping and waiting. There was a sense of expectancy. Something unique was about to happen. And it did!

Passages to read

Luke 24.44–53.
Philippians 2.5–11.

A thought to ponder upon

The ascension of Christ is his liberation from all restrictions of time and space. It does not represent his removal from earth, but his constant presence everywhere on earth.

(WILLIAM TEMPLE, 1881–1944)

A prayer to use

> Risen and ascended Lord,
> you showed us the right way of living.
> Give us grace to follow your example
> of obedience and love.

The gift of the Father

> But you will receive power when the Holy
> Spirit has come upon you; and you will be
> my witnesses in Jerusalem, in all Judea
> and Samaria, and to the ends of the earth
>
> (ACTS 1.8)

The expectancy level among the disciples of Jesus was high. It was some days since Jesus had left them to return to his Father. They had been commissioned to continue the work he had begun but were told to wait until they received the power to do the job. Their work would not be effective without the empowering of God. So they waited patiently for God to fulfil his promise to send the Holy Spirit upon them.

They were not disappointed. Indeed, they were overwhelmed as, with signs and wonders, the gift of the Father was given to them. The house where they were all gathered was suddenly filled with the sound of a rushing wind, tongues of fire appeared above their heads and they began to speak in other languages. It was no ordinary experience. It was no ordinary day. In the Jewish calendar it was the Festival of Pentecost, the feast of firstfruits which included the dedication of the first sheaf of the wheat harvest. In God's calendar it was marked as the day when he would send the Holy Spirit on his Church to fill it with power, life and creativity for its work of witness in the world.

His coming simply couldn't be ignored. Those gathered in the house were filled with the Spirit and began to speak in other languages. Those outside, who had come to Jerusalem for the festival, were filled with amazement. They came from a variety of countries and districts yet each heard his or her own particular language being spoken by the disciples as they told of the mighty work of God. No interpreter was needed. The Holy Spirit enabled the disciples to communicate effectively across the language barrier.

Visitors to Jerusalem were perplexed, not knowing what to make of it. Others were cynical and suggested those in the house had had too much to drink. However, when Peter stood up to speak he left them in no doubt as to the explanation. What they saw and heard was the result of God fulfilling his promise to send his Holy Spirit. It was a promise made to the Jewish people centuries before but only now, as a consequence of the death, resurrection and exaltation of Jesus, could it be fulfilled.

Peter's words, spoken in the power of the Spirit and highlighting the work of Jesus, had a dramatic effect upon his hearers. Many of them became followers of Jesus. Indeed, the reaction of the crowds must have reminded the disciples of those heady days when the popular appeal of Jesus was at its height. Perhaps they were beginning to understand more clearly the promise he had made them, 'I am with you always, to the end of the age.' It was slowly dawning upon them that the Holy Spirit had come, not to make up for the absence of Jesus, but to intensify his presence among them. With the coming of the Spirit, Jesus seemed closer to them than ever before. 'I will not leave you orphaned,' he had said to them. 'I will come to you' (John 14.18). At Pentecost he did so in a very special way and, for the followers of Jesus Christ, life has never been the same again.

The growth and influence of the Christian Church from such humble beginnings relate directly to the work of the Holy Spirit who is the power of God within creation and human life. He brings about transformation, enabling what would be impossible in human strength alone. He inspires and empowers people, equipping them with gifts for service in the Church and in the world, and helping them to live and speak in such a way as bears witness to the risen Christ. The impact of the Spirit-filled Church was such that even opponents referred to the followers of Jesus as, 'These people who have been turning the world upside down.' The Spirit was also instrumental in turning the Church 'inside out', for those who had formerly huddled together within the confines of Jerusalem were soon driven out, as it were, by the Spirit to be witnesses in the wider world.

There is something wonderfully apt about God's choice of the Festival of Pentecost to send his Spirit on the Church. It was the feast of firstfruits. So also was the coming of the Spirit. Just as the dedication of the first sheaf of wheat at the Pentecost Festival was a 'down payment' or foretaste of the harvest that was coming, so the Holy Spirit is the first-fruits or 'down payment' of our future inheritance as God's children. The future is God's and through his Spirit he brings evidence of that future into the present and allows us to share it. With the coming of the Spirit we have already begun to anticipate and enjoy God's tomorrow.

Passages to read

Acts 2.1–11.
Romans 8.12–17.

A thought to ponder upon

No generation can claim to have plumbed to the depths
the unfathomable riches of Christ. The Holy Spirit has
promised to lead us step by step into the fulness of truth.

(CARDINAL JOSEPH SUENENS, QUOTED IN
WARD AND WILD, 1997)

A prayer to use

God our Father,
through the gift of your Spirit
lead us into your truth for today,
that we may be contemporary witnesses to Jesus Christ.

The story continues

Let us run with perseverance the race
that is set before us, looking to Jesus the
pioneer and perfecter of our faith, who for
the sake of the joy that was set before him
endured the cross, disregarding its shame
and has taken his seat at the right hand of
the throne of God.

(HEBREWS 12.1–2)

One of the things I enjoyed most as a bishop was preaching
in ancient church buildings on the anniversary of their

dedication. I always found it a salutary and moving experience. Salutary because, invariably, I was put in my place, reminded that I was but a link in a very long chain. Moving because of the recollection that multitudes of my brothers and sisters in Christ had prayed, worshipped, and kept the faith alive in that place for centuries.

I rarely missed the opportunity to remind the congregation that not only were they linked to those who built that church, perhaps 800 years ago, but also to those who witnessed the resurrection and were foundation members of the early New Testament Church. Indeed, I couldn't keep the note of excitement out of my voice as I recalled that they were linked with the people of God in the Old Testament and, in the eucharist, worshipped with 'Angels and archangels and all the company of heaven'. Wow! That's some pedigree! But it does mean that God began his story a long time ago; a story that still goes on and we are included in the plot.

The story, which began before the world was created and which will end only when God decides to draw all things to himself, has its focus in Jesus Christ. His death and resurrection provide the pivotal point. He not only separates time, he divides history. His coming marks the beginning of a new age. And by the sending of the Holy Spirit God has enabled some aspects of the age to come to impinge on the present moment. When, for instance, barriers of prejudice and sectarianism are broken down, when peace replaces conflict, love conquers hate and healing overcomes brokenness, there the Holy Spirit is at work and God's future is anticipated.

To be honest, however, the story has not always been a pleasant one. Some aspects of it, parts of the Old Testament for instance, are both embarrassing and puzzling. And some other features of the story, especially in medieval times, have done little for the reputation of Christianity and even cast doubts on the character of God as love. There have been periods and episodes in the history of the Church in past centuries that are shameful and call for penitence and sorrow. We do nothing for the integrity of the story of faith if we fail to acknowledge the 'down beat' as well as applaud the 'up beat' aspects of it.

Nevertheless, the story still goes on. Over the centuries, of course, there have been many key players in the story. The patriarchs, the prophets and the apostles all have had major roles to play, as have many so-called 'giants' of the faith since New Testament times, like John Wesley, Martin Luther King and Mother Teresa. But multitudes of unknown and unsung disciples in every age, including our own, have also played their part and the story of God would be incomplete without them.

People are the words with which God tells his story. So, for better or for worse, we have a share in it and can claim it as our story too. It is God's story but it is also a human story which is why, on occasion, it suffers from the weaknesses and failings of humanity. It is a measure of God's trust, that he commits to us the task of being story-keepers and story tellers.

The Spirit that God sent on his Church at Pentecost is a missionary Spirit. Those who receive the Holy Spirit become witnesses. By their words and actions they help to keep God's story alive and contemporary. The majority of people who come to faith today do so because the story of God has become contemporary and made visible to them through the life of a friend or acquaintance. There is no more powerful witness to the Gospel than one which is embodied in a human life. That, surely, is a lesson we learn from the incarnation of our Lord.

It is also one of the great privileges and responsibilities of being a follower of Jesus Christ. However insignificant we may feel ourselves to be, he invites us to be a part of his continuing story for the well-being of his world. He is fashioning a new humanity out of the most unlikely human material, just as he did when he called his first disciples. He trusts us, just as he trusted them, to make his story ours and to tell it by the way we live our lives.

The story continues. On we go. Alleluia!

Passages to read

Hebrews 11.
Hebrews 12.1–2.

A thought to ponder upon

People are the words with which God tells his story.

A prayer to use

All through this day, O Lord, may I touch as many lives as thou wouldst have me touch for thee; and those whom I touch do thou with thy Holy Spirit quicken, whether by the word I speak, the letter I write, the prayer I breathe, or the life I live.

Epilogue

This little book was inspired by the recollection of a cross of stone that still stands on the bank of the River Shannon. At its heart, however, has been a cross of wood that once stood on a hill called Calvary. Across the various aspects of the life and ministry of Jesus Christ, as outlined in its pages, there lies the shadow of the cross.

The incarnation did indeed bring joy to the world but at a cost. Jesus was born to be King but he wore a crown of thorns. His baptism marked the beginning of his public ministry but it also foreshadowed his painful, though purposeful, death. The transfiguration was a very special experience for Jesus and those who accompanied him to the mountain but its pivotal point was the conversation about the cross in the context of glory. The footwashing in the upper room was an acted parable of the cleansing of humankind that he would accomplish through the crucifixion. His lifting up from the tomb in resurrection and his lifting up into heaven in exaltation were indications of God's approval of his life of perfect obedience which culminated in his being lifted up on the cross to die. And the gift of the Holy Spirit came as a direct result of that same lifting up by which both the Father and the Son were glorified.

The cross is central to God's purposes of love for his

whole creation. It reveals the foolishness of God that is wiser than human wisdom, and the weakness of God that is stronger than human strength. Jesus had complete confidence in the attractive power of the cross – 'I, when I am lifted up from the earth, will draw all people to myself.'

In our journey of faith with Jesus Christ we may be led into all kinds of wonderfully exciting experiences that speak more of Easter Day and Pentecost than they do of Good Friday. Some of us, however, may have to pass through wilderness experiences of loneliness and desolation that speak more of crucifixion than they do of resurrection. When God is near we need to thank him. When he seems far away we need to trust him. Whether we are passing through times of joy or times of sorrow we must be careful not to stray too far from the cross. It is the measure of his amazing love – a love which will never let us go and from which nothing in the whole of creation will ever be able to separate us.

O Jesu, Master Carpenter, who at the last through wood and nails purchased our whole redemption; wield well your tools in this your workshop, that we who come to you rough-hewn may be fashioned to a nobler beauty by your hand; for your name's sake, O Jesus Christ our Lord. Amen.

References

Anglican Hymn Book. Church Society, London, 1965.

'Christmas Vespers: Western Rite', *The Oxford Book of Prayer*. Oxford University Press, Oxford, 1985.

Counsell, M. *Prayers for Sunday*. HarperCollins, London, 1994.

Farrer, A. *Said or Sung: Pray Every Day*. Collins, Glasgow, 1976.

Hymns for Today's Church. Hodder & Stoughton, London, 1982.

Manson, T. W. *The Teaching of Jesus*. Cambridge University Press, Cambridge, 1931.

Mission Praise. Marshall-Pickering, London, 1990.

Peachey, J. R. (1896–1971). Copyright the Revd Mary Joy Hancock, with permission.

Ward, H. and Wild, J. *Human Rites*. Mowbray, a division of the Continuum International Publishing Group Ltd, London, 1997, with permission.